INDIVIDUAL
COUNSELING
SKILLS AND TECHNIQUES

Mei-whei Chen
and Nan J. Giblin
Northeastern Illinois University

Lee Hoffman

LOVE PUBLISHING COMPANY®
Denver • London • Sydney

Published by Love Publishing Company
Denver, Colorado 80222

Library of Congress Card Catalog Number 200109282300

Copyright © 2002 by Love Publishing Company
Printed in the U.S.A.
ISBN 0-89108-288-3

CONTENTS

PREFACE

We feel privileged to write this book. For us, words are magic. We have been drawn to the verbal profession—the counseling profession—because we believe in the healing power of words. When said in compassion and from our inner truth, our words have the power to heal, expand, renew, and empower ourselves and others.

This book is about therapeutic language. It is about breaking down step by step the mystique of therapeutic language into various skills and techniques. Counselor trainees often learn a wide range of theoretical frameworks of counseling, diverse ways of assessment and evaluation, and various approaches to pathology development. They have a pretty solid abstract understanding of the clients' struggles. Yet, they often feet inadequate when facing their clients. "What do I actually say to my client?" they often so nervously ask. This book aims to fill the gap that exists between the theoretical knowledge and the actual practice. A central focus of this book is to provide numerous examples to illuminate the gist of each skill and technique.

We have put much energy into crafting the exact ways in which therapeutic messages can be put into words. This book, however, does not concern wording and phrasing alone. Behind each skill and technique, there is a therapeutic end that counselors and therapists want to achieve. Remembering the essence behind each skill and technique is pivotal.

The presentation of the skills and techniques in this book parallels the stages of the counseling process. This book follows the path from the more basic and less intense to the more complex and intense. We start with the skills of intake. Intake is an important skill that is often overlooked in counseling textbooks. After intake, we move through the many empathic skills and onto the advanced skills. This book covers two levels of counseling skills: Chapters 2 through 5 and 8 are suitable for use in a basic individual counseling class, whereas chapters 6, 7, and 9 are especially suitable for an advanced individual counseling class.

We are honored to bring an enrichment to the areas of advanced skills, intervention techniques, and case conceptualization. These three areas usually get little coverage in counseling textbooks. In this book we strive to magnify each of them. In advanced skills, we fan out on advanced empathy, immediacy, confrontation, feedback, and process self-disclosure. In intervention techniques we touch on narrative steps, "Empty Chair" dialogue, reflexive questions, part dialogue, the "Yes" set, and the "No" set. And in case conceptualization, the methods of theme analysis, contextual analysis, unique outcome analysis, and preferred outcome analysis are explored.

We also have provided many specific examples, including session samples and excerpts of trainee journals, which give a glimpse of trainees' psychological journeys through the learning process.

This book draws heavily on our own practices and on our own experiences in teaching, supervising, and giving workshops to students and practitioners at various levels of training. We have been careful to ensure the anonymity of the clients in those clinical examples illustrated in this book.

The process of writing this book has been a journey concretizing our own beliefs about counseling and our basic trust in the importance of the therapist-client relationship. It is through this relationship, which is based on mutual trust and on the counselor's ability to trust himself or herself, that skills and techniques become the vehicle for lasting change in the client. Writing this book has been a growth experience for both of us as we enter the midpoints of our professional careers. It has given us an opportunity to pause and examine our beliefs about counseling and about ourselves. This process of reflection serves as a foundation for our further commitment to and practice of our beloved profession.

Acknowledgments

We wish to thank our students, supervisees, and clients who often teach us more than we teach them. Our thanks especially go to Mr. Stan Love, the publisher, who gave us the privilege of sharing our insights with a broader audience. Our thanks also go to our editor, Erica Lawrence, for her patience and professional assistance. We cannot thank our families enough for their encouragement and support. Finally, we would like to thank our cats, who often serve as a constant source of inspiration and amusement.

CHAPTERONE

THE CHALLENGES OF LEARNING COUNSELING SKILLS

Mastering counseling skills can be one of the most exhilarating turning points in your life. Financial reward is obviously not the reason why people choose to become professional counselors. The desire to help is. Counselors are people born with a passion to reduce mental and emotional suffering in others. This passion to help can be made into a living reality after you master the skills of counseling. To learn counseling skills, however, you need to first change many of your response styles. This process is exciting, and at the same time, challenging. Many challenges face beginning counselors. Among these are (1) the language challenge; (2) the challenge of learning counseling stages; (3) the challenge of peer counseling; and (4) the challenge of overcoming ineffective response styles. This chapter addresses each of these concerns. All the issues dealt with in this chapter, however, are interrelated. It is our hope that the language of counseling illustrated in this book will equip new counselors with competency across the various stages of counseling. All these skills used together move beginning counselors toward professional confidence and mastery.

THE LANGUAGE CHALLENGE

When counselors begin to learn counseling skills, they face two language challenges. First, they need to learn the language of counseling which differs in important ways from routine conversation. Second, they need to learn the succinct speaking style necessary to move clients forward.

The Counseling Language

The first challenge — the counseling language. The language used in counseling is profoundly different from the language we use in our daily social interaction. In social interactions, people listen with the intent to reply. The language in social interactions, depending on what is in the speaker's self-interest, can be vague, evasive, self-promoting, opinionated, lengthy, competitive, intriguing, surprising, funny, chatty, small-talking, effortless, dominant, or subjective. In counseling, however, counselors listen with the intent *to understand and to convey understanding*. The language in counseling therefore must be concise, precise, objective, functional, empathic, thematic, specific, sensitive, respectful, non-judgmental, and accountable.

The shift of language from the social mode to the therapeutic mode presents the most difficult challenge for beginning counselors. The shift in language mode demands a lot of energy, self-monitoring, self-correction, and conscientiousness.

Learning the language of counseling is, in fact, similar to learning a foreign language. For example, beginning counselors may hesitate to speak because they feel that their counseling responses are not natural. Counseling responses may seem foreign or taboo to new counselors who are used to speaking the old language of conversation. Also, just as learning a new language requires starting from simple phrases and moving to more complicated phrases, counselor trainees need to begin with basic counseling language and continue to develop more sophisticated counselor-client responses.

The Succinct Speaking Style

The second challenge — the speaking style. Beginning counselors tend to use some speaking styles they carry from their past. These distracting speaking styles may include:

rambling
using too many fillers
circumscribing
abstracting
elevating tone in the end of a statement
rehearsing
speaking too fast
using a monotonous voice
intellectualizing
domineering
directing

Beginning counselors may or may not be aware of their speaking styles. Yet these speaking styles negatively affect the counseling process. When beginning counselors start to realize their distracting styles and try to change, they face a great challenge because it is difficult to change habitual styles. It is only when counselors have gained expertise in dealing with the language challenges in counseling can they then begin to learn the more advanced skills, such as case conceptualization.

THE CHALLENGE OF LEARNING COUNSELING STAGES

The counseling relationship, like any relationship, goes through stages. Each stage has its own unique developmental tasks and required skills. An amazing number of new counselors, however, are not aware that counseling occurs in stages. Too often new counselors try so hard to solve clients' problems before they have any ideas about who the clients are. They may not even have established rapport with the clients. Their desire to help comes from a good intention, yet their hard work only leads to defeat. New counselors, therefore, need to be aware of the counseling stages, which can be described as follows:

Stage 1: Initial Stage (Problem Exploration)

- Conducting a thorough intake
- Explaining the counseling process to the client
- Establishing rapport (focusing on client's experiences and emotions)
- Reassessing the central problem (focusing on client's actions and failed problem-solving attempts)
- Looking for client's resources and strengths

Skills often used in this initial stage are reflective listening skills: reflection of feelings, paraphrasing, affirmation, perception checking, periodical summarization (see Chapter 3), focusing, probing, and clarifying statements (see Chapter 4).

Stage 2: Middle Stage (Awareness Raising)

- Helping the client develop an emotional awareness of ineffective coping patterns
- Helping the client work through resistance
- Helping the client accept, own up, and honor old patterns
- Helping the client recognize forgotten strengths
- Helping the client envision preferred outcomes

Skills used in this middle stage include reflective listening skills, and particularly the influencing skills such as advanced empathy, self-disclosure, gentle confrontation, feedback giving, immediacy, and reflexive questions (see Chapter 6)

Stage 3:Later stage (Problem Resolution)
- Helping the client see alternative ways of behaving/coping
- Helping the client reach preferred outcomes
- Helping the client implement action of choice

Skills used in this later stage include reflective listening skills as well as influencing skills, and particularly intervention techniques. These intervention techniques may include: Directives, part dialogue, empty chair technique, body awareness technique (see Chapter 7), coaching/teaching/training (assertive training, communication training), role rehearsal, art work/body movement, psychodrama, and other specialized techniques.

Specialized intervention techniques drawn from different theoretical approaches can be applied to the counseling process in this working stage. Counselors need to expand their repertoire of intervention techniques through continued education and personal pursuits.

Stage 4: Termination
- Helping the client evaluate progress
- Helping the client anticipate future happenings
- Helping the client bring closure to therapy

Skills used in the termination stage include all levels of skills.

Please note that the pairing of the counseling stages with certain counseling skills is primarily done for training purposes. A skilled therapist would not restrict himself or herself to basic empathic skills and inquiry skills in the initial or problem exploration stage of counseling. More likely, a skilled therapist in the early encounter with clients may use a combination of basic and a few advanced skills such as advanced empathy, self-disclosure or reflexive questions (see Chapter 6). Please consult Appendix A – Session Samples – and see how certain advanced skills are actually used in the initial stage of counseling.

Also note that the counseling stages are not linear: clients may move back to a stage that has already been explored. For example, a client may have resolved a problem concerning how to deal with her husband. The counselor may even feel the client is ready to terminate, when a crisis event in the life of the client may propel her back into the middle stage of counseling where she has to again examine her understanding of the situation. In other words, the movement through the counseling stages may be recursive.

THE CHALLENGE OF PEER COUNSELING

Counseling skills can only be learned through face-to-face live practice. Richly embedded in the exchange of words are dynamics, emotional tone, non-verbal cues, facial expression and so forth. Learning these skills necessitates face-to-face practice. There is no short cut. Who would be the willing recipients for beginning counselors to practice their newly acquired skills? Certainly not formal clients in the conventional sense. To resolve this dilemma, counselor training programs have relied on peer counseling for skill training. In peer counseling, a trainee is typically assigned to a triad in which each member takes turns as the counselor, the client, and the observer in the lab. This triad may be maintained throughout the process with the same threesome or it may change somewhere in the middle of the term.

If the threesome is maintained throughout the process, you, when role-playing the counselor, will have a chance to see different stages of counseling unfold before your eyes. You will also have the chance to practice advanced influencing skills when the working alliance with your client is well established and when you are able to see the depth and complexity of your client's struggle.

When you role-play the client, you will be able to use this opportunity to work on some personal growth concerns. However, it is this demand — that of being a client — that can provoke some anxiety for you. To resolve this problem you can begin by role-playing an imaginary client; it may be easier initially for you to explore problems using the identity of someone else. Role-playing is less threatening and allows you to ease yourself into the role of the client. This approach may be useful at the beginning of the training process.

Role-playing, nevertheless, cannot last. A role-playing client deprives the counselor of genuine emotions and dynamics to deal with. Role-playing also deprives you of the precious opportunity to put yourself in the client's seat — the flying and, at times, unsettling, emotional experience of exposing yourself, being understood, being challenged, or being enlightened with fresh perspectives. On the other hand, using real problems in the lab gives you some direct experiences of being a client yourself. Then, when you face real clients in the future, because you have been there, you can appreciate some of the misgivings or apprehensions that they might face in talking to a relative stranger about the intimate details of their lives. Therefore, it is wise for you to use this training process as an opportunity to look at some of the real problems or concerns in your own life, especially issues that may influence your effectiveness as a helper. However, counseling is a voluntary act. You set your own pace. When you feel more comfortable and able to trust both this triad and the supervision process, you can work on your own real issues.

Your self-disclosure, however, should always remain appropriate to the goals you set for yourself. You should take some care in choosing what you are going to reveal about yourself. Prepare what you are going to say. Reflect on the impact of the session afterwards. This will prevent you from revealing things that you would rather not.

THE CHALLENGE OF CHANGING YOUR RESPONSE STYLE

The first step in learning counseling skills is to become mindful of your response styles. A response style is the pattern and habit in our communication with others. Long (1996) points out eight response styles that are most commonly used by people in routine communication. Out of these common eight styles, only one is effective in communication and in counseling. Please examine the following eight response styles (Long, 1996), and ask yourself which of these styles you typically use in your daily communication with others. Become self-observant of the impact that your response style has on the person you come to contact.

1. One-Upper
The one-uppers talk as if every conversation is a competition about who has the upper hand. And of course, what happens to others has to be less significant than what happens to them. If someone says he twisted his ankle, the one-upper had his leg broken. No matter what others say, the one-upper has to top it with an account that is smarter, bigger, or more dramatic. If you always manage to get the spotlight of conversation to come back to what you have to say, you may be a one-upper. One-uppers generally try to win control. They are not concerned about the perspective of others or acknowledging others' rights or feelings.

Example:
"You had a bad day? Well, listen to mine."

2. Discounters
The discounters can discredit others' experiences and feelings ever so subtly. Though they don't top others' story with a better one of their own, they discount others' feelings and experiences with indirect put-downs, sarcasm, or reassurance. As a result, others tend to feel small and insignificant. The discounters' responses reflect that they judge rater than respect others.

Examples:

Put-downs:
> "You need to learn to put things in a better perspective."

Sarcasm or joking:
> "If you want to sit here and complain the whole hour, that's fine with me."

Reassurance:
> "I'm sure you'll feel better in the light of day."
> "Oh, people in transition often feel that way."

3. Expert

The expert implies authority and power differentiation. This kind of power differentiation may be real or imagined. The expert could treat you as a parent would a child or as a boss would an employee. The assumption is that the expert knows more than others. If you talk as if you have an answer for every problem that others are facing, your response style might be the expert type. This kind of communication style make others feel patronized because it comes from a position of command, control, judgment, and rescuing.

Examples:
> "I think you are making a serious mistake by not considering your husband's opinion."
> "You have a pattern of never letting yourself have what you want."
> "Stop thinking that way. It is just making you unhappy!"

4. Advice Giver

Advice givers differ from the experts in that they don't operate from a position of authority. Still, they tell others what to do, using key words such as "should" and "ought." Advice giving is the most common response style in our society. It is easy to fall prey to this style. The habit of advice giving is deeply ingrained inside of us, for we think we are doing good to others by giving them advice. In telling others what to do, we rescue others, and unknowingly disempower them. However, the advice givers are the ones who get blamed when the advice doesn't work. Advice givers also reflect control, judgment, and rescuing.

Examples:
> "What you should do is be less self-centered."
> "You ought to sit down and think about the pros and cons of your decision."
> "You should be more self-disciplined in every aspect of your life."
> "You must get control of your emotions."

5. Cross-Examiner

Cross-examiners ask question after question. This series of questions may be designed with the good intention of getting information. Asking question after question, however, gives the cross-examiner a sense of control over the interaction. This communication style can make the other person feel like he or she has done something wrong and is now being interrogated. The cross-examiners gain even more control when they use closed questions. Closed questions differ from open questions in that they allow only for short answers. The cross-examiners don't seem to care about the feelings and perspective of the other person. They can come across as controlling, judgmental, rescuing, and blaming.

Examples:
   "Were you surprised when she did come home?"
   "Have you thought of divorcing her?"
   "Did you tell her how you feel?"
   "Did you feel hurt by her action?"
   "Have you thought of why you are always attracted to this type of women?"

6. "Canned" Counselor
Canned counselors talk like they care but, inherently, they are more concerned about their own perspective. They seem to be empathic, but there is a phony veneer hiding their real attitude of judgment. Canned counselors may appear to say the right words, but later they use the other's reports to judge and evaluate them. They don't come across as authentic and respectful. Rather, they appear judgmental and insincere. You and I can easily slip into this kind of response when we only pretend to be emotionally and mentally present with the person in front of us.

Examples:
   "So how does that make you feel?"
   "I understand how you feel."
   "I have been there myself."
   "I hear you."

7. Problem Solver
Problem solvers imply that they know others' problems as well as the solutions. Similar to the advice givers and the experts, the problem solver's implied message is that others are unable to solve their own problems. This kind of problem solving response never allows others to learn their own problem solving skills. As the old proverb goes, "Problem solvers give others fish, but don't teach them how to catch their own fish." Eventually, the receivers are disempowered. The problem solver may combine cross-examining and advice-giving when they provide their solutions. Again, they are only concerned about their own perspective. They can come across as controlling, judgmental, and rescuing.

Examples:
   "So have you thought of going back to school to better your career choice?"
   "Have you thought of taking a long vacation?"
   "The more you are an introvert, the more often you have got to go out."

"Helping others is the road to personal happiness."
"What have you done for yourself lately?"

8. Empathizer

Among the eight common communication styles, this is the only effective response for interpersonal connection and for counseling. The empathizer strives to understand the other person's perspective and helps the other person discover his or her own inner truth. The empathizer listens attentively and reflects back what the other's true struggles or feelings might be. Even when the empathizer has to ask a question, it tends to be an open-question or a reflexive question. The key is that empathizers put themselves in the other person's skin and feel the other person's world. To do this, the emphasizers have to suspend their own judgments. This response style certainly requires a lot of mental presence and energy. But the empathizers let their respect, authenticity, and responsiveness shine through.

Examples:
"It sounds like you're really feeling lonely and you wonder if that feeling will ever change."
"You are asking me what to do, and I can sense your feeling of urgency to take back a sense of control of your life."
"As I hear your story, I sense that you are beginning to mourn the loss of your childhood and the dream of a loving family."
"It seems you have come to a transition of your life. You want to move forward, but you are afraid of what might happen if you do."
"Let's imagine that there was something that he was resentful about, but did not want to tell you for fear of hurting your feelings, how could you convince him that you are strong enough to take it?" (Reflexive question)

After reading these eight styles, what's your reaction? Among the eight styles, which types do you find yourself using most often?

If your response styles have a tendency to belong to the first seven types, then you may want to ask yourself:

- "Does my current response style help me accomplish my goal of building rapport with the people I work with?"
- "How can I alter my habitual use of the undesired style?"
- "How can I cultivate a more empathic response when talking to others?"

Many people can give you feedbak regarding the first question. Open yourself to listen to this feedback. The answer to the second question is related to that of the third question. When you learn a more effective response style, the undesired style will subside. The two do not co-exist. They obviously suppress each other. All skills and resources in this book are devised to help you develop a repertoire of effective response styles.

SUMMARY

This process of learning counseling skills is exciting and challenging. Its emotional experience can be likened to traveling through the jungles (Barker, 1985). In traveling through the jungles, you doubt at times whether you will ever see your final objective. In learning counseling skills, you will at times doubt whether you will ever feel confident about your counseling skills. In the jungles, you will not be able to invent a route that will get you to the final objective quickly and easily. In learning the skills, you will be frustrated with the slowness of progress and the lack of a short cut. This frustration is normal. While you want to get to the final result as quickly as possible, it is usually best to see your journey as steps. Fix your eyes on the scope of tasks within each small step. Take your journey one step at a time, and you will eventually see the end of the jungle. Appended in the back of the book are many beginning counselors' journals written during this journey. Consult these journals (see Appendix B) when you stumble on the path. Their insight will provide you, as if to climb up a tree and survey your route, with a view of your next landmark.

CHAPTERTWO

INTAKE AND
PROFESSIONAL DISCLOSURE

The counseling process goes through stages. The foundation for the initial stage of counseling is intake. What is an intake? Many beginning counselors ask this question. An intake is the first interview designed to find out basic information about clients' presenting problems, the history and background of the presenting problems, their family systems, coping skills, their functioning levels, strengths, and the goals they want to achieve during the course of therapy. In some mental health agencies, all intakes are conducted by a specially trained staff member; in others, all counselors may take turns conducting intakes. After the intake is conducted, the client may be assigned to an appropriate counselor.

Why does an intake need to be done prior to the start of any counseling work? An intake is done to prevent us from seeing the clients too narrowly, from diving too quickly into clients' presenting problems without a view of the context within which the clients operate. Without an intake, you may see the tree and miss the forest because you don't have enough information to grasp the whole picture of a client's life. You would know only what the client chooses to tell you and miss out on important information that the client does not know is important to tell.

Usually you ask clients to come in 10 minutes earlier, before the intake, to fill out a "preliminary information form" (See Appendix C—Journal Writing—for a sample). This form helps collect clients' demographic information and provides a preview of clients' concerns. Various check-lists are often used here. When the preliminary information form is complete, you give the client a professional disclosure statement. After clients read through your disclosure statement, then invite them in to start the intake.

This chapter discusses the details of intake procedures, including:

- Professional disclosure
- How to do an intake
- Setting goals with clients in the intake
- After the intake

PROFESSIONAL DISCLOSURE

To fulfill the ethical code of informed consent, counselors need to make available to clients all information related to counseling prior to the beginning of counseling. Professional disclosure statements exist for this purpose. As the first integral part of intake, a professional disclosure statement should be given to all new clients to read. A professional disclosure describes who you are to the public. This includes your beliefs, counseling style, and counseling skills. You should also include your titles, licenses, and educational background. Usually, you would include your fee schedules, insurance information, and cancellation policy. Ask your client to sign the statement, indicating that he or she consents to counseling (Keel & Brown, 1999).

In addition, clients have the right to know what happens in therapy, how long the therapy is expected to take, what modes of therapy are available, how long sessions last, how the therapist can be reached in an emergency, or how an appointment should be cancelled. Concerning confidentiality, clients should be told what kind of records you keep, who is allowed to read these records, and what are the conditions under which you may need to breach the confidentiality. Concerning money, clients need to know the cost for each appointment, the time fees should be paid, and what happens if the bill is not paid (Zuckerman, 1997).

The following is a sample professional disclosure statement. You can tailor the statement to fit your situation.

SERVICES DISCLOSURE BROCHURE
NORTH SHORE COUNSELING CENTER

Welcome to the North Shore Counseling Center. We appreciate your trust and the opportunity to be of help to you. This brochure is designed to inform you about our counseling services. As you read it, please feel free to mark any places that are not clear to you or write any questions that come to your mind so we can discuss them during our first meeting. This brochure is yours to keep and refer to later.

What to Expect in Counseling

In counseling, you as a client set the agenda. Initially, you discuss with us your reasons for seeking assistance; together you and your counselor decide which approach is most appropriate to meet your needs. Any personal concerns may be explored in counseling. It is important to realize that nothing is "off limits" to discuss. We are here to work with clients who have experienced a wide variety of difficulties and struggles.

Most clients meet individually with their counselors on a weekly basis, each session lasting for 45 - 50 minutes. As you talk with your counselor, you may begin to see more clearly your feelings and needs; you may develop different goals or motivations for yourself. In working with you, we strive to help you understand yourself, develop greater self-confidence, define your preferred direction, or develop a greater awareness of the needs and styles of other people. Within the counseling relationship, we help you work toward overcoming anxiety or depression, understanding substance abuse problems, or improving your interpersonal relationships. Often, clients who come in to deal with one particular concern decide to continue counseling to work on other issues. You may experience this kind of change in perspective during the counseling process.

Confidentiality

Counseling requires an open and trusting relationship in which you can feel safe to talk about whatever concerns you. In order to safeguard this, the information you share in counseling is treated with the strictest confidence. All therapists are ethically obligated, however, to breach confidentiality in cases where you report child abuse or potential harm to yourself or others.

We may keep intake notes and progress notes about our work together. These notes will be kept in a secure, locked drawer and will be kept confidential as mandated by our ethics codes. We may occasionally consult with each other within the Counseling Center. In such cases, only the information necessary to achieve the goals of consultation or supervision will be shared.

If you have any questions about the confidentiality of counseling information, please feel free to discuss them with us.

Your Responsibility

We can help you only if you are willing to receive help, attend regularly scheduled sessions, and try new ways of thinking and action outside the counseling setting. You are responsible for keeping your appointments. Regular attendance is important for successful counseling results. If you cannot keep an appointment, please notify the Counseling Center at least 24 hours in advance.

The Counseling Staff

The counseling staff is composed of professional counselors with a variety of backgrounds, skills, and interests. Our training comes from the fields of counseling, counseling psychology, or clinical psychology. All of us hold doctoral or master's degrees in these fields of study. If you are interested in knowing about your counselor's training and background, please feel free to discuss this with your counselor.

Equal Opportunity

You have the right to counseling services without prejudice as to person, character, belief, or practice.

INFORMED CONSENT FORM

I have read the Services Disclosure Brochure of the North Shore Counseling Center. I understand my rights and responsibilities in the counseling relationship and agree to abide by them. I understand that all information I share in counseling will be kept confidential except in cases of child abuse or potential harm to myself or others. I hereby agree to participate in counseling provided by the North Shore Counseling Center.

Signature

_____

Client signature   Date

(Please return this page to the Center).

HOW TO DO AN INTAKE

The specific procedures and requirements of intake vary depending on the setting. For example, Adlerian centers often take elaborate family configuration histories in intakes. For beginning counselors, however, there are two simple goals to remember: by the time you have completed an intake, you should have (1) obtained some crucial information from your client and (2) established the basis for a good working alliance (Morrison, 1993). In intakes, counselors use a lot of probing. To establish a basis for a good working alliance, however, you need to make sure that appropriate empathic skills (in Chapter 3) are used to balance the probing. Overuse of probing without empathy skills may make you sound cold and intrusive, so clients feel interrogated.

As a beginner, you may not be able to complete the intake information in one session, so you need to prioritize your focus. Try to get the whole story as early as possible in your working relationship with your client. And remember that no matter how complete your intake is, certain vital information is sure to escape your attention. So you need to maintain a curious attitude and continue to add new observations and information into your original data base. Intake never ends.

It is also important to remember that you will be perceived to be more professional if you pay attention to your dress, grooming, and manner. Try to dress one level up from your clients. For example, if you work in a university counseling center where most clients wear blue jeans, or if you work with adolescents and children, you want to dress casually but with style, not in business suits. However, if you are working with professional people who wear suits, you need to dress as they do if you want to have their respect. If uncertain, go for the more formal style.

Specifically, how does a counselor do an intake? The following are our suggested steps:

Explain the Process of an Intake

1. Before you meet the client, read any information you have about the client (front desk survey, case notes from other professionals)

2. When you meet the client, you need to introduce yourself, state your status, offer to shake hands, indicate the seating arrangement you prefer, and be sure to pronounce your client's name correctly.

3. If you happen to be late for the interview, acknowledge it with an apology.

4. Don't try to start with small talk even though you want, with your best intention, to ease your client. It is better to go right to the heart of the business (Morrison, 1993). If you really need to start with small talk, ask a question that demands more than a yes-no response. Example: "How was the traffic coming here?"

5. Especially for those who are first-time clients, indicate what the intake will be like: how much time it will take, what sorts of questions you will ask, and so forth. Convey some ideas about the sort of information you expect your client to give you. For example:

   "We have about 45 minutes together for today. I want to explain to you a bit about what we will be doing during this time. This is an intake session. I will not be doing actual counseling with you today, but rather, I will ask you many questions just to gather basic information. Many of the questions may be very personal. Please feel free not to answer any questions that you don't feel comfortable with."

6. Convey confidentiality and the limit of it. For example:

   "I understand that it takes a lot of courage to come to counseling. And I want to ensure you that everything that you reveal in the course of counseling will be kept strictly confidential. However, there are some limitations. If you tell me that you are going to harm yourself or another person, or if you tell me about incidents of child abuse, we counselors are obligated to notify the proper authorities. Is this OK with you?"

7. In most cases, during the intake, you will want to take notes or do tape-recording. So point out to your client that you will be taking notes, and make sure that this is all right. If your client feels uncomfortable about your note-taking or recording, explain your needs for it (tape-recording is for educational purpose and sometimes for supervision). If the client still resists, then comply with the client's wishes. Transcribe from your memory later. You want to complete the interview, not win a power struggle. So create a comfortable and safe environment that gives your client as much control as possible.

8. If you will be taking notes, you might say something like this:

   "By the way, during this time I need to jot down some basic information that give me. Otherwise I may not remember all the important information you tell me. The information will be put within your chart, and again, it is kept confidential. Is it okay with you?"

   Nevertheless, you should try to keep note-taking to the minimum. This way you can maintain eye contact with your client, and take more time to observe your client's behaviors and expression. So jot down only key words.

9. If you will be tape recording, you might say something like this:

   "Do you mind if I tape our intake session? The recording is for supervision purposes. It is for us to better serve you. Again, the information will be kept confidential. But if you don't feel comfortable, we will honor your request not to tape the session."

10. Begin tape-recording, only after you get client's permission.

Determine the Presenting Problem

After explaining the process of intake, you can launch into probing the presenting problem that has brought the client into counseling. In probing the presenting problems, you need to learn the specific impact of the problem on the client's life, including emotional distress, physical distress, and the frequency of the distress. Some questions might include the following:

> **"Ok, now can you tell me what brought you in to see me today?"**

> **"How does this problem affect you personally?"**

> **"How does the problem affect you physically?"**

> **"Could you give me some examples?"**

> **"How long have these distresses been going on?"**

Be sure to follow clients's stories with empathic responses (see Chapter 3).

Determine the History of the Problem

After you get a sense of what the problem is, you need to find out the history or background of the problem. You can ask:

> **"When did the problem start?"**

> **"How long has it been happening?"**

> **"What usually tips off the problem?"**

> **"Did you ever have this problem before in your life?"**

Learn the Coping Patterns

Now find out how the client copes with this problem. You may ask:

> **"Have you ever tried counseling or therapy before?"**

> **"What have you tried to solve the problem?"**

> **"How do you cope with the distress caused by this problem?"**

The following is a check list of popular, yet unhealthy, coping habits used to cope with emotional or physical distress:

- Alcohol and substance abuse
- Caffeine addiction
- Compulsive shopping
- Compulsive working
- Nervous habits (Nail biting, facial tics, hair-pulling, foot tapping, finger drumming)
- Overeating

- Being over-responsible (Busy taking care of others, but neglecting oneself)
- Smoking
- Withdrawal
- Passivity
- Victim thinking (Blaming)
- Inactivity
- Others

Check Other Issues or Emotional Concerns

Find out if there are other issues or concerns that the client has not yet covered. You may ask:

> **"Are there any other things going on in your life that I need to know about?"**

Now, summarize the presenting problems and the history before shifting gears to obtain further background information.

Family of Origin Relationships Profile

Now transition to the more intimate phase of the intake concerning the client's family of origin. Provide reassurance that you don't probe into things beyond what the client is comfortable sharing at this time. You might say something like:

> **"I've got a sense of the problems that are bothering you. Now I would like to shift gears to get to know a bit about the family you grew up in. Some of the questions I will ask may be very private. Please feel free to not answer any questions that you consider to be too personal."**

Or

> **"Now I understand what caused you to come here today. Next I would like to talk with you about your childhood and your family. If you don't want to answer any of the questions, feel free to tell me that and we will just move on to a different topic."**

Or

> **"Now I need to understand how you fit into your family. I'm going to ask you some questions about your mom, dad, sisters and brothers (if you have any). This information will be helpful to me to understand the bigger picture, but if you don't want to talk about certain things, just tell me."**

Probe for simple descriptions of family members:

"Could you tell me a little bit about each of your family members?"

"Who are you most like in your family? Who are you least like?"

"Could you describe each of your family members in one sentence?"

Explore the relationships between family members and impact of different family members on the client's current life.

"Which of your family members do you talk to the most? Which do you talk to the least?"

"Could you draw a picture of your family members doing something together? Now tell me about the picture."

"Who in your family do you like the most? Who in your family would you miss the least if that person moved away?"

You might wish to ask specific questions about a client's
- relationship with father
- relationship with mother
- relationship with intimate partner
- relationship with authority
- relationship with self
- relationship with work

Family Mental Health History

Probe for the history of family mental health:

"Have any members of your family been seriously depressed or had some other mental health problem?"

"Have any members of your family been hospitalized for mental illness?"

"Do you recall hearing of any stories of people in your family who might have had mental health problems?"

Personal Resources and Strength

It is important to know the talents and resources clients have that can be mobilized to help them solve their problems. These resources can be uncovered by asking questions such as the following:

"What talents do you have that could help with this problem?"

"Tell me things about yourself that make you proud?"

"Are there any people in your life who are a positive influence on you?"

"What things do you do well?"

"What support systems do you have in your life?"

"What do you do to relieve stress?"

Final Summarization and Explanation

Summarize the major points presented by the client, then explain the next step in the counseling process and verbalize respect for the client.

"Thank you for sharing with me the pain you have been through. I respect your wisdom to take the courageous step to come into counseling. The next session will be the first actual counseling session when you will start working on the solutions to your problem."

At this point you may need to explain procedures or processes. For example, you might need to clarify that you may not be assigned to counsel this client, and that the client should not feel abandoned when assigned to another counselor.

"At our agency, we take turns talking to clients the first time; however, the person who interviewed you may be your assigned counselor. Therefore, if I don't turn out to be your counselor, please don't be offended. It's just the way the agency works."

SETTING GOALS WITH CLIENTS IN THE INTAKE

At the end of the intake, it is common to begin to define goals with the clients. Goal setting is a process that goes on throughout the counseling process. Successful counseling is attainable only if the counselor and the client both start with clearly defined goals (Haley, 1976). Otherwise there is no way of measuring success. Further, the goals must be defined in such a way that the counselor and client can each see clearly whether the goals have been achieved (Barker, 1985).

According to Barker (1985), "many people come to therapy with negative goals. They want to feel less depressed, or to stop eating so much, or to stop smoking. Or they want their children to stop fighting, or their teenage daughter to cease refusing to eat the food they provide. These are all good reasons for seeking professional help, but they are not adequate as outcome frames" (p. 67). A description of the goals "requires more than a statement of what you do not want to be happening." Rather, it is critical to get "a comprehensive picture of how you do want things to be" (p. 67). So it is important to ask clients to elaborate their goals in positive terms, rather than negative terms:

"If you don't want to feel depressed, how do you want to feel?"

"What will replace smoking (or eating) in your life?"

"What will your children be doing if they are not fighting?"

Even when clients' goals are stated in positive terms, they are frequently vague and ill-defined. For example, clients may say that they want to "feel happier" or "have more energy" or "be able to decide what I want to do with my life." Barker (1985) pointed out: "such statements are all right as starting points for the discussion of treatment goals, but they are not in themselves adequate outcome frames. What does 'feel happier' mean? Happier than what or whom? Under what circumstances does the person what to feel happier? How will the client and the therapist know that the desired degree of happiness has been achieved" (p. 68)? So it is important to get the client to describe, in as much detail as possible, how things will be when counseling is successfully concluded. For example, to the client who said he/she wants to feel happier, we may ask:

"When you feel happier, what would you be doing exactly?"

"When you have more energy, how would you act differently from now?"

"When you are able to decide what you what to do with your life, what will your life be like?"

In short, therapists need to guide clients to state their goals in behavioral and realistic terms. In this way, the client's and the therapist's energy can be channeled into well-defined focus.

AFTER THE INTAKE

After the intake, the therapist and the client start working on the presenting problems stated in the intake interview. The presenting problems are usually not exactly the core issues, but they are good starts. Presenting problems can be seen as trial balloons; they are presented by clients as experimental issues.

If we take the presenting problems seriously, clients will later proceed to share more profound concerns ingrained deeply inside themselves.

People long to focus on exploring their problems. So don't be afraid to explore clients' issues from all different angles. The guiding principle of the first session after the intake is "start small." Solving even one minor problem can lead to improved confidence and a chain reaction of success.

On a practical level, the following are possible guidelines to consider in the first counseling session after the intake:

- Start with the summary (see Chapter 3 Section 5) of the client's presenting problems. In the summary, it is better to organize the presenting problems into many sub-categories.
- After the summary, focus one area of concern that needs immediate attention.
- Listen to the client's focused problem in more detail. Respond with empathic skills, such as paraphrasing, reflection of feelings, and summarization (see Chapter 3).
- Explore how the presenting problem impacts the client's emotional, intellectual, or physical life.
- Explore what solutions the client had attempted but failed.
- Explore what has stopped the client so far from making the desired changes.
- Explore the client's resources and strengths.

Remember, these guidelines are not rigid steps. Often, they are interwoven in the flow of the session. How to flow from one exchange to another in the session is really a clinical judgment. Please see Appendix A—Session Samples—for how the exchanges between the counselor and the client flow in the session.

Officially, a counselor needs to keep "progress notes" (see Chapter 9 Section 5 - How to write case notes) for the client after each session and secure them in the client's chart. As a beginning counselor, you may want to keep "process notes." Process notes differ from progress notes in that they are kept for the counselors benefit only. They are usually informal reminders to the counselors, therefore, they are not filed. Process notes serve to remind you of areas that you might want to explore in the following session, or ideas that you have had about how to conceptualize the client's case. They can be jotted down as a drawing, a chart, or as key words for unchecked insights. See Chapter 9 for how counselors usually conceptualize the case.

CHAPTER THREE

BASIC EMPATHY: REFLECTIVE LISTENING

People want to be heard. People want to find someone who really knows and understands what they are going through. And yet, many people seem to have a hard time revealing their true thoughts and feelings to others. It's difficult to open up. To break down this communication barrier, we need to use the technique called "reflective listening" or "empathic listening."

Many beginning counselors feel compelled to offer solutions when their clients are just starting to present their problems. You need to strive to avoid this sense of mission. When clients start to tell their concerns and problems, what is most important is for the counselor to make the clients feel heard and validated. Clients don't want people to try to fix their problems right away. When they feel heard and validated, clients open up more.

You make clients feel heard and validated through the use of empathy. Empathizing is not mimicking what the client says. Mimicking is parroting; it is an insult to the client and it frustrates the relationship. Rather, empathizing means sensing what clients feel without their saying so, or reading clients' emotions even when they are unspoken. Clients rarely express what they feel in words; instead they use tone of voice, facial expression, or other non-verbal cues. If you can tune in to the unspoken, you will be more in touch with the moods of your clients. Your ability to sense these subtle communications builds the connection with your clients. When your clients' feelings and meanings are heard and validated, the empathic responding itself becomes therapeutic and healing.

Use reflective listening skills throughout the counseling process and you will find how anxious your clients will be to open up to you when you help them feel understood. Reflective listening skills even work with clients who are normally withdrawn and incapable of open communication.

Remember three principles when you practice reflective listening:

1. You must not provide opinions regarding your clients' attitudes or feelings. Don't evaluate! Don't even sympathize! Any opinion that you express, even when it is positive, may cause clients to close down. Why should we not show sympathy for our clients? Because even sympathy is a type of judgment. Your sympathy tells your clients that you have stopped listening and started to evaluate. Giving sympathy to clients, even if given with your best intentions, will cause them to doubt your objectivity.

2. Don't push! Don't try to dig for information that your clients may not be ready to reveal. Let your clients reveal themselves to you at their own pace. This non-threatening atmosphere, where your clients can express themselves at their own pace without fear of criticism and judgment, is priceless for your clients. This kind of patient listening is rare in their lives. Seldom are people able to give others such a deep sense of being understood.

3. Don't give advice! When you give advice to your clients, what it implies to them is that you don't think they are capable of figuring things out for themselves. This can be extremely demeaning. Nevertheless, clients will still ask you "What should I do?" Don't drop your guard! What they really need is for you to reflectively listen to them. Knowing what to do has never been a problem for most clients. The real problem is that they have a subconscious conflict about actually doing it. Telling them what they should do only enhances their sense of conflict, guilt, and most importantly, resistance toward you. So save your breath and advice.

The more reflective listening you provide your clients, the better the rapport or therapeutic alliance that will be created. The importance of reflective listening as a clinical tool cannot be emphasized too much. It is perhaps the most essential skill of all in your clinical repertoire. Commit these reflective listening skills to memory. Practice them in your relationships with others. You will remarkably increase your influence with your clients. Practice it every day!

Listening and responding at this highly attuned level is a demanding process: you need to put aside your own emotional agenda temporarily so that you can clearly receive clients' signals. At the same time, you cannot shut down your own perceptions. You must recognize your body's own signals for emotions. For example, when listening to your client, you might feel a tightening in your throat. This tightening needs to be heeded because it may be a response to what the client has said. Perhaps the client feels a tightening in her throat. Perhaps what the client said has triggered some emotional issue from your past. Or perhaps you are restraining yourself from telling your client something that you assume would better be left unsaid. Whatever the reason for your internal responses, it is important that you are aware of them so that you can use the messages of your body to help the client. It might be that the client is causing your throat to tighten in anger or frustration. Perhaps other people react to your client in the same way. So by paying attention to your bodily reactions, you get the first-hand experience of how other people react to your client. These are the messages that you may want to note for future reference.

You may want to keep your observations of your bodily reactions to yourself if it is early in the counseling process. In later sessions, it might be beneficial to the client to share your reactions using the advanced skills in Chapter 6.

It bears repeating, empathic listening and responding is a demanding process. To put aside your own emotional agenda temporarily, and at the same time, to recognize your body's own emotions may seem foreign. Indeed, giving empathic responses is no less demanding than speaking a foreign language. When you are learning a foreign language, you have to be open and willing to be vulnerable. In the same vein, when you are truly empathic in your listening and responding, you open yourself up to influence. That is, you become vulnerable. To influence clients, you need to do two things: first, you must be willing to be influenced, and second, you need to be aware of how you are influenced when it happens.

The prerequisite for empathy is self-awareness.

Empathic response provides the cornerstone for all later interventions. Empathy functions as a bridge between counselor and client. Forming an empathic connection with clients is imperative in achieving therapeutic reconstruction of client problems (Neimeyer, 1996). As Teyber (1997) states "It is the relationship that heals. The relationship between the therapist and the client is the foundation of the therapeutic enterprise" (p.16).

At the technical level, empathizing is a process that involves two parts: active listening and reflective responding. In active listening, the counselor listens with intent to understand, to get inside the client's frame of reference. In reflective responding, the counselor decides what words to use to capture client meaning, and what feelings to affirm to reflect client experiences.

Reflective responding employs a number of skills that are discussed in this chapter. They include:

- Minimum encouragers
- Paraphrasing
- Reflection of feelings

- Affirmation
- Summarization
- Perception checking
- Reflection of meaning
- Pacing

The following sections explore these various forms of empathic listening and responding skills in details.

MINIMUM ENCOURAGERS

Minimum encourages are the signs that let the clients know that the counselor is present and breathing. They, however, are not the epitome of empathic responses. Minimum encouragers are only interpersonal lubricators; they, in themselves, are not therapeutic. Minimum encourages are short phrases that can be used throughout the counseling process when the emotional level of the session is not extremely intense. They are low-key responses, and overuse is not encouraged.

Don't overuse minimum encouragers. Minimum encouragers do nothing more than lubricate the dialogue. They do not convey deep understanding and therefore do not usually move a client's exploration to a deeper level.

Using Minimum Encouragers

Minimum encouragers can be grouped into four categories:

- Minimal habitual verbal utterances

  "Um-hum."

- Repetition of key words

  "Complicates it?"

  "Angry?"

  "Trouble getting along?"

- Short Restatement (repeat back short phrases)

  "You got angry."

  "You have trouble getting along with your boss."

  "You are not sure what you should do."

- Short Confirming Comment

A short confirming comment lets clients know that you are following what they are saying and that what they say makes sense to you. These comments help clients understand that their behaviors are human nature. For example, grieving clients often think they see a deceased loved one standing beside them when they wake up in the morning. This is a normal grief reaction. If the counselor makes a short confirming comment, such as **"Many people also have the same experience,"** the client will feel much better. The following are other examples of short confirming comments:

> **"I understand what you mean."**
>
> **"That certainly makes sense."**
>
> **"That certainly explains a lot."**
>
> **"Sometimes that happens."**
>
> **"Many people also have the same experience."**

The Impact of Minimum Encouragers From the Client's Point of View

Clients feel encouraged to go on with their stories, although they do not know how deeply the counselor understands them.

PARAPHRASING

To paraphrase is to restate in a succinct form (1) *the cognitive aspects of what a client brings forward,* or (2) *the point a client wants to make.* Repeating what clients are saying is not paraphrasing. Rote repeating is plagiarizing what clients say. It does not earn points for the empathic connection between counselor and client.

Using Paraphrasing

A true paraphrase may contain at least two elements, but other elements may be added.

- A sentence stem

> **"Looks like you are saying . . . ."**
>
> **"I hear you say that . . . ."**
>
> **"As I hear you, it sounds like . . . ."**
>
> **"Let me see whether I catch the situation . . . ."**

- The basic message of the client

An example of paraphrasing might proceed as follows:

Client:
"My feelings do not matter to anyone; 1950's women do not voice their opinion. Because I am not providing an income, I can't express my thoughts."

Counselor:
"As I hear you, it seems that your being unemployed is having an adverse effect on you."

Here are some other examples of paraphrase responses:

"The point you're trying to make is that you spend too much time on planning; you do this so you can feel in control."

"Sounds like on one hand you love him, but on the other hand you wonder if you can ever really get along."

"It seems that you are finding it difficult to do your job satisfactorily and, at the same time, to cope with the problems caused by your daughter and your wife's poor health."

"So you are concerned about what to do to help your daughter."

"So you don't think your boss is fair."

Note: Paraphrasing seems a bit artificial at first for the beginning counselor. After a while, it feels like a more natural form of communication than the usual questions, opinions, or bland conversation fillers.

The Impact of Paraphrasing From the Client's Point of View

Skillful paraphrasing has a number of positive results:

- Clients usually feel understood as a consequence of counselor's paraphrasing.
- Clients tend to like the counselor who paraphrases skillfully.
- Clients tend to feel encouraged to go on with their stories as a consequence of paraphrasing (Brammer & Macdonald, 1996).

REFLECTION OF FEELINGS

One powerful way to convey empathy is through reflection of feeling. When your clients pause for some response from you, you briefly describe their feelings even more accurately than they themselves have articulated. You reflect their feelings back to them. This helps your clients more clearly identify their own feelings, and at the same time gives them a sense of connection with you. For example:

"Sounds as if you are upset because your boss is overly critical."

"So he is quick to criticize you for trivial things, while totally ignoring your positive contributions."

In reflecting these feelings, you demonstrate to your clients that you understand what they are experiencing, and you communicate the message that "I am with you. I can sense the world that you are feeling and perceiving."

Unfortunately, reflection of feeling is not a skill that many people are born with. You need to learn it. It takes tremendous effort to become proficient at this valuable skill. Learning to reflect feelings is similar to learning a foreign language, learning to play a musical instrument, or learning to draw. All these skills require training, practice, and critical review of one's work (see Appendix D—Counselor Self-Critique, and Appendix E—Observation Charts), which when done in a disciplined fashion produces an artist. In a sense, counseling is an art. Counseling skills and techniques can be taught. But only through self-discipline and self-knowledge does a counselor become a true artist.

Using Reflection of Feelings

To effectively reflect clients' feelings, you need to be alert when they speak.

• Notice nonverbal expressions

Sometimes a client may not tell you how he/she feels, yet from nonverbal expressions, you can get a sense of the client's feelings.

• Listen to verbal messages:

Constantly ask yourself internally:

"What are the *core* messages?"
"What *themes* are coming through?"
"What is most important to him or her?"
"What does he or she want me to understand?"

Withhold your instinct to formulate responses. Simply listen.

• Listen to the client in context.

Pay attention to the circumstances that trigger clients' feelings and responses. This helps you put your feet in the clients' shoes, enhancing your ability to see where the client's feelings and responses come from.

● Keep your observations in your mind. Withhold confrontation.

When you listen to your client's story, you may notice something. You may notice the way in which the client exaggerates, contradicts, or misinterprets reality. When you do, keep this information and your observations in your mind for later hypothesis testing (after the end of the session, you may want to jot down your observation. This is the situation where process notes may be useful). *Don't judge your clients. Don't confront your clients at this point. Don't interfere with the flow of the dialogue.* The right to confront can only be earned when you have established a secure, trusting relationship. The trusting relationship is established through your accurate reflection of client feelings and your total acceptance of your clients.

You can use two types of reflection to reflect your clients' feelings. These are:

✔Using lucid feeling words to reflect feelings
✔Using metaphors or analogues to reflect feelings

The following sections explain both these methods and give examples of how you might use them.

Using Lucid Feeling Words to Reflect Feelings

When you call a feeling by its name, such as "anger," "hurt," "guilt," or "joy", you help your client identify it more clearly and recognize it more deeply (Hanb, 1991). Simple reflection of feelings can do a lot more than you might realize. Many beginning counselors feel that it is necessary to say a lot so that clients know they are being understood. Often, however, a counselor who can just name a feeling for a client opens up a whole new avenue that the client has never explored. Naming feelings often inspires clients to take a new view of the situation. Consider the following examples:

Client:
"The VCR in the school is missing. Well, two teachers came up to me and said 'What did you do with the VCR?'"

Counselor:
"So you are angry; you feel blatantly accused."

Client:
"I am not sure that this counseling profession is for me. The other people in the program seem to be catching on faster than I am. Others seem to be picking up the knack of empathy faster than I. I'm still afraid of responding directly to others, even with empathy. I have to re-evaluate my ability to stay in the program."

Counselor:

"You're feeling pretty inadequate and down, perhaps even enough to make you doubt your choice of this new career."

Client:

"It's like I don't know who I am any more. I never really accepted this part of me before, it is starting to come out. It seems like I am a new person."

Counselor:

"It sounds like you are afraid of the changes that are happening to you."

Client:

"I don't know, sometimes life just seems too hard to go on."

Counselor:

"I hear exhaustion and hopelessness in your voice."

Client:

"And although I have finished the project and done a good job, I didn't feel happy about it at all."

Counselor:

"Although you have all the reason to celebrate your success, you feel numb."

Following are a few more examples of using lucid feeling words to reflect. You should note that these examples are counselor responses. The client's prompts are not included here; however, you can see that every counselor calls the client's feelings by name. The feeling words are exact.

"On one hand you feel excited about moving out, and on the other hand you feel guilty for leaving your Mom alone."

"When you are not in control, you feel nervous or disturbed."

"You are very upset, and feel hurt very badly inside."

"You appear to be feeling angry at this moment toward your parents."

"Right now, you really are angry with him."

"I have the sense that you are angry, but you feel you are not supposed to be."

"You feel dejected because you can't express your thoughts to your husband."

"You seem rather guilty when you sense any hint of sexual feelings."

"I have the sense that you are angry at your mother but you think it is awful of you to feel that way."

"I'm getting a sense that you feel hurt when he doesn't call. It's not easy to talk about that, and I'm pleased you have found a way to get to it."

Using Metaphors or Analogies to Reflect Feelings

Metaphors and analogies are comparisons that help clients link their inner experiences with a visual image. Clients, thus, experience their feelings in a more tangible and powerful way.

"When you study hard and then fail the exam, you *feel like punching a hole in the wall.*"

"You feel as if there is nothing you can do about the inequalities in this situation. *You feel as if you are beating your head against a wall.*"

"So, when your mother-in-law comes to visit, *you feel a loss of freedom, hemmed in . . . like an animal in a cage.*"

"When you practice really hard and lose the match, *you feel like kicking a pile of bricks.*"

"When you heard your father say that, *it felt like a slap in your face.*"

"It is like you feel you're *coming undone" (losing control).*

"You feel like you are on cloud nine" (excited).

"You feel as if you are going to explode" (furious).

"It seems that you feel like you are moving mountains" (having great difficulty).

"You seem to feel that there is nowhere to turn" (helpless).

"So you feel like you're skating on thin ice" (nervous).

"You feel like you are walking on a tight rope" (nervous).

"It is as if you feel you are at the end of your rope" (hopeless).

"There is a sense that you feel like a pile of manure" (worthless).

What to Reflect

To help clients experience and own up to their feelings, you should reflect how *they* feel rather than reflect how *others* make them feel. For example,

"It sounds like what she said made you feel irritated."
(This is other-centered reflection. Avoid it!)

"It sounds like you feel irritated at the things she said."
(This is client-centered reflection. Do this!)

"I can see that she annoys you."
(Other-centered. Avoid it!)

"I can see that you feel annoyed around her."
(Client-centered. Do this!)

Exception:

Using Normalization of Feelings When Working With Minority Clients

Openly discussing feelings and emotions may initially feel foreign for some non-white clients, especially Asian/Pacific islanders. For these particular groups, restraint of feelings and reservation of emotional expression are culturally sanctioned behaviors (Sue, 1990). It is possible that counselors' uses of reflection of feelings may seem intrusive to them. However, counselors still can help these clients feel validated when they use *normalization of feelings.*

To normalize clients' feelings is to acknowledge that those feelings they experience have often been felt by others who were in similar situations. Normalization of feelings gives these clients permission to bring their feelings and emotions into the open. It also helps clients not feel alone or abnormal.

To normalize clients' feelings, you can say:

"A lot of people in this situation would feel insulted. Is this how you feel, too?"

"I would feel exploited if my boss treated me this way. Is this how you experience the situation, too?"

Avoid Question-Disguised Reflection

Take care that you are doing nothing more than reflecting clients' feelings.

"Do you feel resentful when your needs are given low priority?" (This is a closed question. Reflection of feeling should not be in question form.)

Now change this closed question to a reflection of feeling:

"You feel resentful when your needs are not his priority. Is this how you feel?" (This is a reflection of feeling + perception checking.)

"You feel very numb this morning?" (Although you are reflecting the client's feeling of numbness, this is not a reflection of feeling. Why not? Because with an intonation raised in the end of sentence, your response becomes a question.)

Suggestions

To effectively reflect clients' feelings:

- **Give yourself time to think before you respond.**
- **Permit yourself to feel.**
- **Use short responses.**
- **Gear your responses to the client, but remain yourself.**

However you must be sure to avoid:

- Questions
- Cliches
- Interpretations
- Advice
- Parroting
- Sympathy and agreement

Remember that empathy is a way of being, not just a professional role or a communication skill. Who the counselor is as a person is more important than what the counselor says. This means that the counselor must be able to open up to the client, to respect the client, to convey unconditional regard, and to acknowledge that the client has the capacity to grow. To do so, try to:

- Set judgments and biases aside for the moment and walk in the clients' shoes.
- Respond fairly frequently, yet briefly, to the client's core messages.
- Move gradually toward the exploration of sensitive topics and feelings.
- Respond with empathy, then attend carefully to cues that either confirm or deny the accuracy of your response.
- Keep in mind that the communication skill of empathy is a tool to help clients hear their own feelings and their problem situations more clearly.

Finally, remember you do not have to be an exceptionally insightful or perceptive person to understand clients' feelings. And you won't and can't be accurate all the time about how they feel (Teyber, 1997). Don't wait until you totally understand your clients' feelings. Don't worry about making mistakes. Don't try to reflect perfectly. Just reflect along the way. Your clients just need to sense that you are making efforts to understand their feelings.

Feeling Words (Ranked by Level of Intensity)

The following list of feeling words is designed to help new counselors who are more cognitively oriented to develop a vocabulary of feeling words. The list is presented in hierarchical order. As you move down the list, the words suggest increasing levels of emotional intensity. Using the words at the bottom of the list involves more risk. It is best in the beginning to use the words at the top of the list. These words are imperative to remember when you use "successive approximations" in advanced empathy (see Chapter 6, Section 1).

Sad	Angry	Anxious
discouraged	annoyed	concerned
down	aggravated	dismayed
low	irritated	timid
downcast	upset	apprehensive
sorrowful	perturbed	anxious
downhearted	insulted	shaky
distressed	indignant	nervous
depressed	resentful	tense
dismayed	mad	agitated
dejected	angry	startled
dispirited	furious	afraid
heartbroken	enraged	fearful
hopeless	infuriated	frightened
helpless	raging	terrified
powerless	incensed	horror-stricken
miserable	wrathful	panicked
numb		
anguished		
desperate		

Hurt	Guilty	Confused
uncomfortable	ambivalent	uncertain
disappointed	at fault	unsure
wronged	blamable	distracted
mistreated	guilty	pre-occupied
offended	culpable	disorganized
insulted	ashamed	puzzled
stung	terrible	perplexed
hurt	awful	bewildered
injured		disoriented
wounded		dazed
disheartened		confused
disillusioned		frustrated
demoralized		
shattered		

Inadequate	Stressed	Unfair
awkward	stretched	unaccepted
embarrassed	tired	neglected
floundered	burdened	judged
hesitant	stressed	rejected
doubtful	strained	left out
inadequate	stressed-out	excluded
incompetent	exhausted	put down
unqualified	overwhelmed	discriminated
unfit	subdued	mistreated
inept	overloaded	accused
a failure	defeated	cheated
	subjugated	betrayed
	dominated	manipulated
	overpowered	exploited
	stifled	violated
	suppressed	
	oppressed	

Happy	Connected	Strong
glad	warm	effective
satisfied	touched	centered
content	moved	focused
happy	empathic	grounded
delighted	sympathetic	resolute
excited	caring	healthy
rejoiced	close	firm
elated	fond	strong
ecstatic	connected	powerful
overjoyed	intimate	potent
exhilarated	loving	solid
blissful	attached	unwavering
jubilant		impenetrable
		indomitable

The Impact of Reflection of Feeling
From the Client's Point of View

- Clients tend to feel that their feelings are validated and accepted.
- Clients feel that their emotions are acknowledged.

- Clients begin to feel they have been seen and are no longer invisible.
- Clients are more likely to trust the counselor.
- Clients are more likely to reveal on a deeper level.
- Clients will be more receptive to the counselor's leads later on.

AFFIRMATION

After you have acquired the skills of basic empathy, you can actively support your clients. When clients feel negative about themselves, a positive remark from you can make a difference. By offering support, you can increase clients' self-esteem and sense of competency in dealing with life's challenges and problems. When you directly affirm clients' inner strengths, you affirm a sense of self-efficacy, so that they feel validated and better able to take responsibility for their lives. For example, just telling a client that she is capable of keeping her counseling appointment might be enough to help the client feel that she is capable of taking care of herself.

Using Affirmation

The following phrases are examples of affirmation:

"I appreciate how hard it must have been for you to go through this."

"I think it's great that you want to feel better and that you are willing to put forth the effort to change."

"You are certainly a courageous person, to have been able to survive with the trauma that you have been through and not fall apart."

"It must be difficult for you to live your life when it is so full of stress. That must be why you are here in counseling to feel better."

"You are certainly having to cope with a lot of problems right now and I understand why you would want to escape from the pain."

"It appears that you have made great strides from being shy to now being totally yourself and opening up."

Effective affirmation requires the therapist to exercise great care. Therapists sometimes confuse affirmation with comments that diminish clients' feelings, thus making clients feel invalidated and insignificant. The following are examples that are not affirmations and should be avoided:

"Don't worry, it will get better."
"Don't worry, it will always get worse!"

"Things are so bad they cannot get worse."
"Why worry. Be happy!"
"Uncle had the same problems and he got over it."
"It will be fine. Cheer up!"
"You are taking this too seriously."
"God never gives you more than you can handle."

The Impact of Affirmation From the Client's Point of View

- Clients feel supported by the therapist.
- Clients get positive affirmation about some aspects of their lives.
- Clients learn to think about themselves in a more positive way.
- Clients observe the therapists modeling self-affirming ways to think.

SUMMARIZATION

Another form of basic empathy is summarization. To summarize is to link together materials that the client has discussed. To summarize is also to keep track of the common thread in the presenting problems and connect the related issues. Linking phrases, such as *"on the one hand .. on the other"* and *"at the same time,"* can be used to tie the related issues together. Summarization is used in four forms:

✔Open-Session Summarization
✔Periodical Summarization
✔Closing Summarization
✔Cross-Session Summarization

Using Summarization

The following sections give examples of the four types of summarization.

Open-Session Summarization

A short form of summary can be used to begin each session, building upon progress made earlier. This often provides a needed sense of continuity.

> **"I've been thinking about our last session when we talked about your many responsibilities for your siblings, job, and graduate school and your lack of time for yourself. I asked you to think about what you would do if you weren't taking care of everyone else. I wonder what you've thought of?"**

Periodical Summarization

During a session, it is helpful to periodically summarize the client's theme. Periodical summarization can help both counselor and client stay focused, which further helps clients explore their core issues in a deeper level.

> **"It sounds like you are torn two ways. On the one hand, you are worried that your drug use is hurting your family, and you are also concerned about all the money you are spending on the drug. At the same time, you certainly don't think of yourself as an addict, and you believe that you can quit the drug any time you want without any bad effects. This must be puzzling for you."**

> **"To sum it up, you are really frustrated in two ways. First, you are frustrated that the system is inadequate to prevent the theft from happening; second, you are frustrated that you are accused of stealing, which you did not do."**

> **"From your talk about marriage, weight, and now your new job, you seem to have experienced feelings of personal failure in all of them."**

> **"There is a lot of pain and confusion in what you have just told me. Let's see if I understand some of the main points you have made. . ."**

> **"You have said quite a bit. Let's see how the pieces fit. Your mother has confided a secret to you and you can't tell your father. You feel stuck in the middle. Is that how you feel?"**

Closing Summarization

At the end of a session, it is helpful to offer a major summary, pulling together what has transpired thus far. In giving such summaries, you must decide what to include and to emphasize.

> **"We have three minutes left. I think this is an appropriate point to sum up what we have covered today. We covered how you want to stay rooted in your fortress even when that home is not safe for you and not comfortable for your wife. Your wife is also not happy about the time and energy that your gang battle takes away from your attention to her. You really love and care for your wife, but to you it is also important to keep up the fight for justice in your neighborhood."**

> **"Let's review what we've accomplished in our session today. How does it appear to you?"**

Cross-Session Summarization

When appropriate, it is helpful to the client when the counselor sums up the common threads that run through different sessions.

> Client:
> "Anytime I start a new relationship I feel really anxious. I just don't have any confidence in myself about keeping the man I am attracted to."

> Counselor:
> **"I wonder whether your lack of confidence has anything to do with your father's emotional unavailability when you were young. You have talked about how your father never was home because he was always at work. I wonder whether the two are related."**

> Client:
> "I never thought of that, but that makes sense."

In this example, the counselor summarized a theme *that had appeared several times previously.* A summarization that points out the thread helps the client gain insight into the connections between feelings. Consider another example:

> **"In the past few weeks, we have reviewed your concerns about your relationship. Some of the following things seem to stand out. You have felt angry and resentful toward your ex-husband and father. You also have felt disheartened and lonely. However, it appears that you have difficulties experiencing those feelings, because when you talk about those feelings, you laugh. Tell me what the feeling is behind the laugh."**

Remember that summarization encompasses different components of an important theme. The following examples show paraphrasing, which is *not* summarization.

"It sounds like no matter what you do, you can't beat this thing on your own."

The Impact of Summarization From the Client's Point of View

- Clients begin to see common themes in their lives.
- Clients learn how to organize their problems into meaningful patterns.
- Clients observe the modeling of the therapist, who connects different ideas that could have been seen as unrelated.
- Clients learn to see therapy as an integrated process rather than as a series of isolated, unrelated sessions.

PERCEPTION CHECKING

In daily ordinary conversation, people often—intentionally or unintentionally—obscure their true feelings. It is common to fear that others will not be accepting or that they cannot be trusted. Social conditioning encourages people to chatter onward, even to deliberately confuse meaning with innuendo, humor, irony, and metaphor. It is rare for people to check with one another about what they intend to say (Brammer & Macdonald, 1996). However, in the counseling relationship, you need to reverse this process and put a heavy premium on direct and clear communication. This clear communication can be achieved through the technique known as perception checking.

Using Perception Checking

Perception checking is verifying with clients that you accurately understand what they are saying or feeling. Often in the counseling setting, counselors' own views and experiences may cloud the actual meanings clients try to express. For example, a client may state that his mother died the week before. The counselor might assume that the client is sad at the loss of the mother, when, in fact, the client may have hated the mother and be glad that he is now free of her control. By using perception checking, you can ensure that you are not forcing your own assumptions on your clients.

On a technical level, perception checking may involve a chain of several skills, such as a paraphrase + a checking, or a reflection of feeling + a checking, or a summarization + a checking. Here, a checking is an inquiry such as "Is this correct?" "Am I right?" "Do I understand you correctly?" or "Let me clarify what you just said."

Perception checking is a higher level of empathy because you are combining an empathic statement with a checking inquiry. This combination makes you sound more astute, but at the same time you are creating a clear boundary between yourself and the client. The client feels embraced by you because of the empathy, but at the same time feels a sense of differentiation from you because of the respect shown in your checking inquiry. Perception checking helps you achieve empathy without the one-upmanship of sounding like an expert. The following examples show how to use perception checking.

> *"If I understand you correctly, you* **are saying that you would be less anxious if your husband would be more reassuring.** *Is this correct?"*

> (The phrase in italics shows the perception checking. Everything else is reflection of feelings.)

> **"You seem to be very angry with your son.** *Is that right?"*

"I was wondering if leaving your husband is the plan you really want. I heard some doubt. *Did I hear you right?"*

"I want to see whether we are on the same page. You said that you want to live independently, yet in the last few minutes you said that you can not imagine leaving your old father alone. I detected strong contradictory feelings toward the move. *Is that the way it appears to you, too?"*

The Impact of Perception Checking From the Clients' Point of View

- Clients are likely to feel understood in a way that is rare in other relationships.
- Clients may feel truly understood for the first time. This is where communication in counseling differs from ordinary conversation.

REFLECTION OF MEANING

Reflection of meaning, like reflection of content and reflection of feelings, is another way to convey empathy. Of the three types of reflection, it is probably the deepest and often the most complex. When you reflect a client's meaning, you are demonstrating that you understand the *significance,* or *importance,* of the material the client is presenting. You are saying that you understand the client's own *personal interpretation* of the matter at hand.

Using Reflection of Meaning

To use this skill, your task is to clearly reflect back to your client what you are hearing and your awareness of the significance from your client's point of view. Although your goal is always to be as succinct as possible with your responses, sometimes it takes more than one sentence to adequately reflect a meaning. When listening to your client's story, be alert to nonverbal expression. Sometimes clients tell you what they think they *ought* to believe or experience, but from nonverbal cues, you may observe their deeper feelings.

When working with clients, constantly ask yourself internally:

"What is most important to this client?"
"What does the client believe this experience says about him or her?"
"What values are being expressed?"
"Are conflicting values making prioritizing difficult?"

Compare current information clients are telling you with past meanings they have articulated, and be alert to patterns and parallels. Don't confuse your hypotheses regarding core messages with the client's own interpretations. Hold your ideas privately and be open to changing and adapting them as you are presented with more data.

Reflect of meaning can be employed in three forms:

✔Reflection of values
✔Reflection of beliefs
✔Reflection of aspirations

Reflection of Values

Values are principles, behaviors, or beliefs that your client finds more desirable or worthy than others. Value conflict might be one of the problems that brings clients to counseling. A client needs to determine priorities when two or more values cannot be served at the same time, and one must take precedence over another. To help clients determine priorities so as to resolve value conflicts, counselors must first reflect back the clients' values. The following examples illustrate reflection of values. In each example, the reflection of values is italicized.

Client:
"I know that I'll enjoy the work they offered me, but I think I'll go crazy if have to sit in a cold little cubby hole with poor lighting, tile floors, and all metal furniture."

Counselor:
"So in evaluating whether or not to take this job, you *realize that the work environment may be as important a factor for you to consider as the job description."*

Client:
"So many people these days just go through the motions in their jobs. They don't seem to care about how well a job is done, just that they get paid for putting in the time. It doesn't seem right to me that people collect a check they didn't earn. I couldn't live with myself if I were like that. Even if no one else caught me being sloppy, I'd know."

Counselor:
"For you, doing a job well is a matter of personal integrity."

Client:
"I don't really care about the personal lives of my students. What they do on their own time is their business. I'm no bleeding heart or crusader out

to save the world. I just want the students to learn what I'm being paid to teach them. I do my job; they do theirs; and that's it."

Counselor:
"For you, what is most important about being a teacher is seeing to it that students learn the subject matter you are presenting."

Client:
"I got the promotion! I was afraid that because I am so quiet, no one would notice me and promotions might be a long time coming. But my boss told me that my quiet steadiness is exactly what they need in someone to head up this project."

Counselor:
"So your work has not gone unnoticed. This evidence ensures you that *being yourself and being successful do not conflict.*"

Client:
"My parents want me to take Latin, but I want to take Spanish. Usually my parents have good advice about courses, but this time, I think they're way off. Which one do you think I should take?"

Counselor:
"Sounds like *you're torn between two sets of values*—to trust their experience or to trust your instincts. It also sounds like *you're hoping that input from me could tip the balance one way or the other.*"

Reflection of Beliefs

Beliefs are conclusions people make about the way the world works. They are rules, real or imagined, that people develop about how things "should" be. These *underlying beliefs form* the lenses through which clients view and give meaning to life events. Reflection of client beliefs bring clarity to the session, helping clients put their unarticulated beliefs into words. Again, the italicized portions of the following examples show reflection of beliefs.

Client:
"I feel horrible. I am going to end up with a B in one of my courses. No matter what I do, I just can't seem to shake the humiliation of it."

Counselor:
"You seem to believe that something is terribly wrong with you if you don't get all As."

Client:
"He's generous, all right. He never denies me anything that I want—within reason, of course. But he's my father, and I need more from him

than just material things. I wish he could understand how I feel about things, and be there for me during this really confusing time in my life. Isn't that what fathers are for?"

Counselor:
"You appreciate your father's financial support, *and it seems you believe that you should be able to count on him for emotional support as well."*

Client:
"I don't know why my wife is making me come here. She's the mother. She's the one who's with the kids all the time. She's the one who's having problems controlling them. I work hard all day, and the last thing I need when I get home is her getting on my case about every little thing that went wrong with her day. Coming here is a waste of my time when what's really wrong is her inability to control the kids."

Counselor:
"Sounds like you believe that the day-to-day challenges of parenting are primarily a mother's responsibility. **And, given your own responsibilities as a father, you find it inappropriate and perhaps even burdensome to come here and discuss problems that you see as hers, not yours."**

Client:
"I just inherited all this money from my godmother. I've never in my life had so much money at my disposal. But after a lifetime of putting the needs of others first—the business, the house, the kids. . . I just can't imagine spending any of that money on myself. After all, there's nothing worse than a spoiled brat. Sure, I could probably use some new things, but I'm not the self-centered type. What would my friends say if they ever found out how rich I am now? They'd despise me!"

Counselor:
"It sounds like you believe that anyone who spends money on their own needs is by definition spoiled and self-centered and deserving of rejection."

Reflection of Aspirations

Aspirations are hopes and dreams. Most people process the data of life by making comparisons between the reality (experienced self) and the aspirations (ideal self). Ordinarily, they set goals, stated or unconscious, that provide a measuring tool for how successful they perceive themselves to be. They ask themselves:

"Am I closer to reaching my goal now than I was then?"

"Am I becoming more or less effective?"
"Are these changes going to be desirable or undesirable?"
"Am I moving toward danger or safety?"

Clients make intense comparisons, especially in times of change and transition. Reflecting the relationship between the client's ideal self (aspiration) and the experienced self can help clients grasp the significance of their experiences. The following examples illustrate client statements that reveal aspirations. The italicized parts of the counselor's responses show reflection of those aspirations.

> Client:
> "I've been coming here for a couple weeks now. And I can already see it's making a difference in how I view conflict. But I still go through so much of my day feeling afraid, and I am so tired of having this weight on me all the time."
>
> Counselor:
> **"Even though you see some evidence of change, you are wondering whether or not you will ever reach *that dream of living free from the burden of fear.*"**
>
> Client:
> "My test scores were so low. I can hardly believe how low. And so much was riding on them. What will I do?"

Skill Differentiation: The Differentiation Between Reflection of Content, Reflection of Feelings, and Reflection of Meaning

- Reflection of content (paraphrasing):
  To restate what the client is thinking and doing.
  "So you are spending a lot of time doing mindless activities."

- Reflection of feelings
  To mirror clients' feelings and emotions without judging or confronting them.
  "Sounds like *you feel anxious* most of the time because you *are bored with* your life."

- Reflection of meaning
  To restate the values, beliefs, or aspirations of clients.
  "It sounds as if you are experiencing a feeling of emptiness because *you are not proud of the person you have become.*"

Counselor:

"Sounds like your scores have really shaken up your confidence, to the point that you are starting to question the possibility *of reaching your dream of making a mark in society."*

Client:

"I am 52 years old and I just found out that my husband is having an affair with a 26-year-old woman. I am at a time at my life when I had hoped to retire and travel with him. Now I find that he plans to divorce me."

Counselor:

"Sounds like *your dream of life-long love and growing old together has been shattered.* And you are wondering how you will put your life back together."

The Impact of Reflection of Meaning From the Client's Point of View

- Clients tend to experience a sense of relief when they feel understood.
- Clients feel as if their concerns are being taken seriously.
- Clients often experience a sense of clarity about their concerns when their values and beliefs are identified in specific situations or dilemmas.

PACING

To pace is to mirror a client's speech pattern. Pacing is a process in which two people selectively attend to each other's verbal and nonverbal communication and concurrently reflect it back to each other. Consequently, pacing happens naturally when the two parties develop deep rapport (Dolan, 1985). In counseling, you match your pace with that of the client if you want to develop a secure therapeutic relationship (or working alliance) with a client. Pacing does not solve the client's problem, but it increases client's receptiveness to your therapeutic interventions (Dolan, 1985). It is frequently used in the initial counseling stage, and less as the counseling process unfolds. However, even in later stages of counseling, pacing may be used when clients experience emotional distress or resistance.

Using Pacing

There are four types of pacing:

✔Topical Pacing: Reflective Listening
✔Nonverbal Pacing: Mirroring the Nonverbal

✔Verbal Pacing: Matching Client's Language
✔Vocal Pacing: Matching the Client's Speech Pattern

Topical Pacing: Reflective Listening

Pacing the client topically means following topics of the clients, without imposing one's own agenda. Topical pacing (Dolan, 1985) conveys a meta-message to the client that "I am with you; I am interested in what you are saying. What you have to say is meaningful and important." *Paraphrasing, reflection of meaning, and reflection of feelings* are three effective methods of pacing clients topically (Meier & Davis, 1993). *Summarization and perception checking* work as well to achieve topical pacing.

Nonverbal Pacing: Mirroring the Nonverbal

Pacing the client nonverbally means partially matching your body language with the client's head position, weight shifts, movement of feet, hand gestures, body movements through space, or body posture (Robbins, 1986). For example, "the therapist might swing her left leg in synchrony with the client's leg and simultaneously match the tone and volume of the client's voice" (Dolan, 1985, p. 67). However, some clients' nonverbal behaviors are uncomfortable, such as breathing rapidly and shallowly. You may not want to select those for mirroring.

Verbal Pacing: Matching Client's Language

When you match a client's language, it tends to convey a subtle meta-message of acceptance and appreciation to the client and reduce possible unconscious resistance (Dolan, 1985). Different people tend to have different ways of perceiving the same situation. Specifically, many clients use their visual faculty to process information, while others may pay more attention to auditory, kinesthetic, or olfactory environmental cues. If you listen to a client's language, you can determine which perceptual set the client is most comfortable with. Then you can adjust your language to fit the client's style. This practice is based on a theory of counseling called neuro-linguistic programming (Bandler, 1979). The following counselor statements demonstrate verbal pacing.

To pace visual clients, use visual predicate words (Robbins, 1986), such as:

"It *seems* that your wife and you don't *see eye to eye* in . . ."

"*Looks* like you are angry by Tom's *view* about your . . ."

"I can *envision* how much hurt you have experienced . . ."

To pace auditory clients, use auditory predicates:

> *"I hear* **you say that your** *voice is not heard* **at your job."**
>
> **"It** *sounds* **like you are perplexed by the** *double message* **in . . ."**
>
> *"As I listen* **to you . . ."**

To pace kinesthetic clients, use kinesthetic predicates:

> **"It is as if** *you feel . . ."*
>
> **"We have** *tapped into* **several new themes. Let's pause for a moment and see whether I understand you correctly. . ."**
>
> **"It is as if what he said** *touched* **a very vulnerable part of you."**

To pace unspecified clients, use general predicates:

> **"I get a** *sense* **that you are not happy with the way your wife is treating you."**

Vocal Pacing: Matching the Client's Speech Pattern

According to neuro-linguistic programming (NLP), you can develop rapport with clients by adapting to the speed, the inflection, the energy with which they speak. For example, if a client speaks rapidly, you may need to perk up a bit to match the client's energy. Conversely, a depressed client who speaks slowly may respond better when you speak softly and slowly. Really, what is being done here is that you are following your client's lead. It is as if you and the client are engaging in a dance, with the client leading and you following.

The Impact of Pacing From the Client's Point of View

- Clients feel that what they have said is meaningful and important to the counselor.
- Clients experience synchronicity with the counselor.
- Clients feel accepted and appreciated.
- Clients feel visible.
- Clients feel an unconscious bond with the counselor.

CHAPTERFOUR

BASIC INQUIRY SKILLS

The initial stage of counseling is the problem exploration stage. To explore the client's problem, you need to use both basic empathic skills and inquiry skills. In chapter three, you learned the basic empathy skills. Now in this chapter, you will learn the inquiry skills. What are inquiry skills? Inquiry skills are used to gather relevant information and to channel the exploration of the client problems in certain directions. The inquiry skills discussed in this chapter include:

● Focusing
● Probing
● Clarifying statements

One word of caution: in inquiring, you are indeed leading clients. By contrast, in reflecting clients feelings (discussed in chapter three) you are following their leads. The client-therapist relationship is like a dance. When you use empathy skills, you follow and the client leads; when you use inquiry skills, however, you lead and the client follows. In the therapeutic dance, there is a fine balance between following and leading. The important point to remember is that you must not overuse or abuse inquiry skills in the initial stage. You can kill the relationship if you ask too many questions.

FOCUSING

The first inquiry skill is focusing. Usually, in the beginning stage of counseling, clients tend to ramble vaguely or cite multiple problems. When they do this, they often feel overwhelmed or confused, and lose their problem-solving ability. Big problems need to be broken down into small pieces and prioritized so that they are manageable. Focusing is useful in this kind of situation to help clients center on specific issues. Focusing is also a good technique to help clients center in on one topic or to identify specific emotions related to a given event. When clients are able to find a focus, a clear perspective may appear more readily.

Using Focusing

The skill of focusing usually starts with an empathic statement and then narrows down to a specific direction the counselor wants to pursue. Two areas that are good candidates for focusing are:

✔Focusing on problems
✔Focusing on feelings

Focusing on a Problem

To focus on a problem, the counselor uses questions to help the client focus on one topic or concern, rather than trying to solve all the problems at once.

Client:
"I want to call my sister and talk to her, but I don't want to talk to the rest of the family. I don't want to deal with the rest of the family right now. I am angry with them about a lot of things."

Counselor:
"I heard you say that you are angry at your family (basic empathy). *Can you elaborate more specifically on whom you are most angry with (focusing)?"*

Some other examples of focusing include the following statements:

"I noticed that you mentioned 'loss of self.' Can you say more of what you were thinking when you said that?"

"John, earlier you said a couple of things. I would like to go back and follow up along those lines with you."

"Please tell me more specifically what behaviors of your son upset you."

"You have been discussing many topics the last few minutes. Could you tell me which topic concerns you most and elaborate on that?"

Focusing on Feelings

Frequently beginning clients talk about events in their lives but are not able to attach feelings to these events. The role of a counselor is to help clients understand what they are feeling in the given situation. The focusing skill can help the counselor accomplish this task. For example:

"We have been talking about what happened to you last week, but I haven't heard you talk much about your feelings yet. Could you name a feeling you have right now?"

"Just now I noticed your expression changed. What are your feelings now?"

"We have talked in the past about your stress levels, but we really haven't explored how you feel under those stressful situations."

The Impact of Focusing From the Client's Point of View

- The clients learn how to focus on one problem or feeling at a time.
- The clients experience less stress because of the focus.
- The clients are able to explore problems more fully and come to clearer perspectives.
- The clients are able to identify feelings and relate to certain life situations.

PROBING (QUESTIONS)

The second inquiry skill is probing. Probing is asking questions that cause clients to look more deeply into underlying features of their problems. Probing can perform three functions. It can be used to (1) gather information, (2) evoke motivation to change, and (3) generate new meanings and experiences.

Using Probing

This section focuses on the first two types of probing:

✔Probe to Gather Information
✔Probe to Evoke Motivations

The third type, reflexive questioning, is covered later in Section 4 of Chapter 7, Intervention Techniques.

Probe to Gather Information

The first type of probing is asking questions that help counselors gather information. This type of probing generally comes naturally to counselors because it is an integral part of everyday conversation. But counselors should seek certain specific information, which they gather by choosing questions that are intended to move the session in a particular direction. The particular direction you want to move is usually toward increased concreteness in meanings and increased clarity in patterns of connectedness.

- Opening an interview

    "**What would you like to talk about today?**"

    "**Could you tell me what has been going on?**"

    "**The last time we met we talked about your tension about _____. How did it go this week?**"

    "**Perhaps we could start by having you telling me where you are now.**"

- Probing for *specificity* and *concreteness*

    "**Could you give me a specific example of what your wife does?**"

    "**What does she do specifically that brings out your anger?**"

    "**What happened first (next)?**"

    "**What was the result?**"

    "**What did she say (do)?**"

    "**What did you say (do)?**"

- Probing for clients' points of view

    "**What do you mean when you say 'depressed'?**"

    "**What do you mean when you say your father is out of his mind?**"

    "**Could you tell me more about it?**"

    "**You say that he is outside of the circle, yet he is domineering (empathy). Could you elaborate on what you mean (probing)?**"

    "**In what way is that a concern for you?**"

    "**Could you give me an example?**"

    "**How else does it affect your income?**"

    "**For example . . .**"

    "**How much does this issue concern you?**"

- Probing for client's internal experiences

    "**What's your feeling that goes with the tears?**"

    "**How did you feel when it happened?**"

    "**How do you feel when your mother yells at you?**"

"Would you like to tell me what is on your mind at this moment?"

"If you had to ask yourself one question right now, what would it be?"

● Probing for meaning

"What does all this mean to you?"

"What kind of sense does this make to you?"

"What do you tell yourself when . . ."

● Probing for missing data

"What important things are happening in your life right now?"

"Is there anything else happening in your life at this time?"

"Any other things that might contribute to this?"

"What were the ways you have tried to solve the problem?"

"What other information do I need to know to understand this problem?"

● Probing for the pattern of connection

"Who else worries?"

"Who do you think worries the most?"

"Who do you imagine worries the least?"

"What does she do when she worries?"

"What do you do when she shows you that she is worrying?"

"Are there any occasions when this pattern arises?"

Probe to Evoke Motivations

The second type of probing goes beyond information gathering. It can induce client motivation for change and growth. This type of probing can be exemplified by evocative questions, extreme questions, and looking-back questions (Miller & Rollnick, 1991). It is also called *motivational interviewing* because the questions as such are designed to arouse a desire in clients for healing and transformation. When used with care and sensitivity, the motivational questioning can propel the interviewing process into a therapeutic and productive direction. Following are some examples of different forms of motivational questioning.

- Evocative Questions

    Evocative questions are designed to evoke clients' concerns about their own problems, leading them to think about why they are stuck with their problems.

    "What difficulties have you had in relation to your drug use?"

    "In what ways do you think you or other people have been harmed by your drinking?"

    "How has your use of tranquilizers stopped you from doing what you want to do?"

    "How much does that concern you?"

    "What do you think will happen if you don't make a change?"

    "What makes you think that you may need to make a change?"

    "What would be some advantages of making a change?"

    "What do you think would work for you if you decided to change?"

    "If you could wave a magic wand and change yourself, what would you change?"

- Extreme Questions

    Extreme questions are those that cause clients to examine the most dire possibilities, forcing clients to look at what they are trying to avoid seeing. Clients are often in denial concerning the results of their behaviors. Extreme questions help clients see the reality of the effect of their continued miscreance.

    "What concerns you the most?"

    "What are your most dreaded fears about what might happen if you don't make a change?"

    "What do you suppose are the worst things that might happen if you keep on the way you have been going?"

- Looking-Back Questions

    Looking-back questions motivate clients to change by examining how much better their lives were before they allowed their problems to control them.

    "What were things like before you started drinking so heavily (or before you started binging-purging so regularly)?"

    "Tell me about how you two met each other, and what attracted you to each other back then?"

    "What are the differences between the Mike of 10 years ago and the Mike of today?"

"How has the use of drugs (or violence) stopped you from growing into the person you dreamt of becoming?"

Suggestions for the Use of Probing

- Do not engage clients in question-and-answer sessions.

Because questioning is a much less demanding skill for the counselor than empathic reflective listening, it is easy for counselors to fall into the question-answer trap, asking a series of questions rather than reflecting the client's statements. Asking too many questions may provoke resistance in clients (Miller & Rollnick, 1991), causing them to become defensive rather than more open with their feelings.

- If a probe helps a client reveal relevant information, *follow it up with basic empathy rather than with another probe.*

  Counselor:
  "What's your mother's attitude about your marrying outside your race?" (Probing)

  Client:
  "She has cut off communication with me."

  Counselor:
  "You must have been disappointed and hurt by your mother's response." (empathy response)

  Client:
  "Yes, I was devastated by her shutting me out."

  Counselor:
  "What was your relationship like between you and your mother when you were a child?" (Probing)

- If you find yourself asking clients three questions in a row, chances are there is something in yourself you need to work on.

  Client:
  "I really don't know how I feel about my husband anymore."

  Counselor:
  "Are you thinking of divorcing him?" (Probing)

  Client:
  "Well, I occasionally think about it, but not very often."

Counselor:
"What situations make you think about divorce?" (Probing)

Client:
"Well, sometimes I think I want more intimacy in my relationship, and when he never listens to what I say, I start to have second thoughts about our marriage."

Counselor:
"What do you think could happen if you divorce your husband and look for what you deserve in another relationship?" (Probing)

In this example, the counselor asked the client three questions in a row, presuming that divorce is an option on the client's mind, when actually divorce may be more of an issue for the counselor than for the client.

● Don't use "why" questions.

It is easy to be critical without even realizing it. A few subtle types of criticism easily escape notice. Using *why* is one common culprit. If that surprises you, try to use the word "why" a few times in a row. But do so at your own risk! The word *why* is interrogative in nature, and it creates an automatic defensive response. By using it, you unintentionally demand your clients to justify themselves.

If you sincerely want to understand your clients' reasons for doing certain things, you can simply say:

"Could you help me understand some of the reasons that lead you to do so?"

"I wonder *what* are the possible *reasons* that make you think this way."

● Don't use close-ended questions.

Close-ended (or closed) questions require minimum response from the client, can usually be answered in one or two words, and may stop the flow of the session. They must be used sparingly. When you find yourself uttering a closed question, stop! Re-word it into a open-ended question or a statement. For example:

Close-ended question:
"Have you ever thought of telling your mother how you feel about the curfew hour?"

Open-ended question:
"What do you think will happen if you tell your mother how you feel about the curfew hour?"

● Don't use strategic questions.

In this mode of questioning, the counselor behaves like a teacher, instructor, or judge, telling clients how they ought to behave.

By asking strategic questions, the therapist/counselor is imposing his or her views of what "ought to be" on the client. The counselor has in mind how the client should behave, and rather than simply telling the client what to do, the counselor asks loaded questions. In other words, the counselor has a hidden agenda in asking the question. That agenda is to subtly convince the clients to change. Of course, sometimes a corrective question is needed to mobilize a client who seems to be in a stuck situation, but too many may disrupt the therapeutic alliance.

The following are strategic questions. Remember that they are not recommended.

"Why don't you talk to him about your worries instead of turning to your kids for support?

"Can you see how your withdrawal causes your wife to become disappointed and frustrated?"

"Is this habit of making excuses something new?"

"What would happen if for the next week at 8 a.m. every morning, you suggest he take some responsibility?"

"Have you thought of asking your husband to get some help?"

The Impact of Probing (Questions) From the Client's Point of View

● Clients get a wider view of their problems.
● Clients are able to explore connections between their behaviors and the problems.
● Clients learn how their attempted solutions for their problems have failed.
● Clients are able to make their problems concrete.

CLARIFYING STATEMENTS

The third kind of inquiry skill is the clarifying statement. Clarifying statements are better than questions in encouraging clients to talk and to explore. Pure questions or probing, as described in previous sections, tend to put clients on the defensive, particularly if the probing is perceived as accusatory. Asking too many questions at once makes the clients feel as if the counselor is cross examining them. The impact of that is that the session feels more like an inquisition than a helping environment.

The purpose of clarifying statements, like probing, remains the same: to gather information. The clarifying statement, however, more gently elicits information from clients' narratives. Indeed, it often helps clients to focus more on their feelings. Clarifying statements make the information gathering process safer and more personable because clients do not build up walls of defense.

Using Clarifying Statement

A clarifying statement involves a combination of a couple of skills: *reflective listening skill* + *not-knowing position*. The combination makes clients feel as if they are heard, but also gathers the information needed by the counselor.

In the following examples of clarifying statements, notice how the reflection and not-knowing position are combined.

> "I can see that you're angry (reflection), but *I'm not sure what it is about* (not-knowing position)."

> "I realize now that you often get angry when your mother-in-law stays for more than a day (reflection). But *I'm still not sure what she does that makes you angry* (not-knowing position)."

> "It seems that you have already begun to think of a plan (paraphrasing). I *am interested in hearing some of your ideas* (not-knowing position)."

> "I understand that you are concerned about your drug use (paraphrasing). *So please help me understand what you enjoy about using drugs and what's the down side of it* (not-knowing position)."

> "I understand that talking to your family is stressful (reflection). But I *am not sure what your family does that makes you feel so stressed and angry* (not-knowing position)."

> "You say that you are 'mean' to your students (paraphrasing). *I'm not sure I understand how you are mean to them* (not-knowing position)."

The Impact of Clarifying Statement From the Client's Point of View

- Clients are helped to reveal more information in a non-threatening environment.
- Clients are able to look more deeply into their patterns and motivations.
- Clients are able to feel more rapport with the counselors.
- Clients feel that the counselor has heard what they are saying and is interested in knowing more about them.

CHAPTER FIVE

HELPFUL HINTS FOR BEGINNING COUNSELORS

S ome common problems may start to emerge after you work with clients for a while. You may find your client loses interest because you talk too much; you may find the client rambles on and on without getting to the point; you may find yourself attempting to fill in silence; or you may find yourself being ineffective in some other way. This chapter offers tips for addressing several problematic scenarios that you may encounter in your practice.

UNDERSTANDING PRESENTING PROBLEMS

The problems clients first present are called "presenting problems." Presenting problems are like trial balloons—they are small, and experimental. It is not that clients don't trust you with their real problems or that they try to mislead you regarding what they need to work on. In fact, clients believe that the presenting problem is their most pressing problem. Counselors need to take the presenting problems as what they are. If these presenting problems are not rejected, clients feel safer about sharing more deeply experienced problems.

The process of counseling usually proceeds from presenting problems to deeper feelings if counselors are effective listeners and if they establish a trusting relationship with each client.

LISTENING TO SILENCE

Silences are a lot harder on beginning counselors than they are on clients. Beginning counselors tend to be tempted to fill silence in the session at all costs, and are likely to start asking questions to get the client talking. It is no accident that beginning counselors ask more questions than experienced counselors. A counselor's intolerance of silence may hinder clients from processing their thoughts and feelings sufficiently (Meier & Davis, 1993).

Sometimes the client is using silence to think, explore, or assimilate some important new feelings, thoughts, or insights. If you keep on chattering, it stops this important processing. If the client is using silence to reflect, your best response is to respect the silence and wait for the client to break it. Most experienced counselors learn to live through silences and see them as constructive. Indeed, sometimes silence can be more revealing than spoken language. However, if, after you have waited a while, your client is still quiet, you can invite discussion again by asking:

> **"I am wondering what went through your mind in this moment of silence."**

Sometimes the client is suffering and embarrassed at not being able to think of anything to say. If this is the case, then the most empathic response you could make would be something like:

> **"There seem to be no words that convey what you are thinking or feeling at this moment."**
>
> **"Sometimes it is difficult to find a language for the pain we are experiencing."**
>
> **"I can tell it is hard for you to know where to start."**
>
> **"Seems like you have exhausted the subject."**
>
> **"You seem to be too tired to talk. I am wondering if you can talk about how your exhaustion feels?"**

Counselors need to listen to client silence in a cultural context. In some non-Caucasian cultures, especially Asian, silence or pausing is not a floor-yielding signal; rather it may indicate "a desire to continue speaking after making a particular point" (Sue 1990, p. 426). A white counselor who is not comfortable with silence may fill in conversation too quickly and hinder the minority client from elaborating further.

Furthermore, silence in Asians sometimes is a sign of politeness and respect. It would be a unnecessary disaster for the Caucasian counselor to misinterpret a minority client's silence as a sign of ignorance or lack of motivation.

DEALING WITH A RAMBLING CLIENT

People ramble in various ways: swamping you with details, adding comments tangential to the issues, or having difficulty knowing when their turn at talking is finished (Schloff & Yudkin, 1991). For clients, rambling could happen for many reasons (Martin, 1983):

- Sometimes rambling is a client defense against the fear of engaging in real contact with the counselor.
- Sometimes it is a well-established defense against painful feelings and thoughts.
- Sometimes it is just a casual verbal wandering due to not feeling present in the moment.
- Sometimes it is the result of a habitually wordy style of talking.

If a client continues to ramble, there will be no therapeutic growth because rambling gets in the way of exploration and self-confrontation. One thing you can do is to keep a mental map of the central issue and understand how the details relate to the key point. When the client rambles, you might say:

> **"Let's stop you for a few minutes to see if I understand what you have just told me. I think this story you are telling me about your father's childhood sort of illustrates what you were thinking before;** *that is, you wish your father had been more present in your life when you were a child.* **Is that what you are trying to say?"** (The italicized part indicates the key point of the client's story.)

> **"Let me see if I can pull together some of the stories you have been talking about. It seems** *that fear of abandonment is a theme that runs through all of your experiences.* **Would you agree?"**

FREQUENCY OF TALKING (COUNSELOR)

On one hand, therapists need to be an active participant in the process of counseling, so the therapist needs to respond frequently to facilitate a client's self-exploration and self-confrontation, using all the skills learned. On the other hand, if therapists respond *too* frequently, they can dominate the process, not letting the client do the work.

The client is supposed to be the problem solver in an active and on-going process. Counseling is more beneficial for the clients if they themselves go through the steps of problem solving. Counselors are supposed to facilitate this process in the client. But if clients have to listen to clever speeches, they will lose the momentum of the exploration process. Your job as a counselor is to hear the essence of the client's message and bring that to life.

How do you do that? There is a easy formula to keep in mind. Counselors should speak about 35%–40% of the time in the session. Not much more, not much less. Monitor your own frequency of talking. If it is too much, you have something to work on. If it is too little, you need to be more assertive to bring the client's core message to life.

TENTATIVE LEAD-IN PHRASES IN REFLECTING

When you make tentative statements, it opens up space for exploration and inspiration. Skillful tentativeness (Martin, 1983) communicates to clients that they are the source of information about their experiences. The client is the final authority on his or her own reality. Skillful tentativeness also gives clients the freedom to correct what the therapist says. Tentativeness can be achieved by beginning sentences with lead-in phrases.

The following are examples of how counselors can begin statements to help clients get to their FEELINGS. The italicized words indicate the tentative lead-ins.

"**I guess** you feel . . ."
"**You seem to feel** . . ."
"**I sense that maybe** you feel . . ."
"**You feel as though** . . ."
"**It is as if you** . . ."
"**You must have felt** . . ."
"**Kind of feeling** . . ."
"**Sort of like** . . ."

The following are examples of how counselors can begin statements to help clients get to their POINTS:

"**It sounds like** . . ."
"**I guess you mean** . . ."
"**I guess you are saying** . . ."
"**I am picking up that** . . ."
"**If I am hearing you correctly** . . ."
"**To me it is almost as if you are saying** . . ."
"**What I guess I am hearing is** . . ."
"**Could it be that** . . ."

AVOID VAGUE THERAPY

Vague phrases often heard in our daily lives are bad options in therapy. Unfortunately, many counselors do vague therapy. By responding in non-specific ways, many counselors make statements that fit all clients in all situations. By using generic statements that have minimal substance, counselors avoid thinking and conceptualizing during the session. This type of vague, global, undifferentiated response doesn't serve clients well. They often further a client's sense of feeling unseen, unheard, or invalidated.

The following phrases may be handy whenever you can't think what to say. But they are not exact enough or specific enough to be therapeutic. They cannot bring the client's experience to life. Although these statements can be used occasionally as short confirming comments (described in the section of Minimum Encouragers, Chapter 3), we recommend that you avoid these vague statements as much as possible.

Don't use the following vague statements:

"I guess you are pulled in different directions about that."

"I understand what you mean."

"I understand how you feel."

"I hear what you said."

"That is something."

AVOID DISCOUNTING PHRASES

Avoid using some phrases that are often used in social conversation. These phrases, although used with good intention, tend to discount clients' feelings rather than to validate them.

"Don't worry about it."

"You will get over it in time."

"That's not so bad."

"Life will go on."

"Time will heal."

"This is nature's way."

"Everything happens for a reason."

"There is something to be learned from this."

"There is always light at the end of the tunnel."

When you don't know what to say, say nothing. Silence is better than discounting phrases. Indeed, silence is golden, particularly in counseling (Meier, 1983).

AVOID INTELLECTUALIZING

Many counselors approach therapy as an intellectual process in which correctly identifying the cause of the client's problem will somehow cure those problems. Indeed, this kind of generalized abstraction (intellectualization) cuts off the client's exploration; it moves the client away from current experiences toward intellectualization (Martin, 1983). Any counselor whose comfort zone is in the cognitive domain needs to make additional efforts to become more empathic if he or she wants to become a more effective counselor.

The following examples illustrate intellectualizing responses. It's easy to see how they arrest a client's exploration.

Client:
"I am a total loser. My family would be better off without me."

Intellectualizing Counselor:
"You certainly sound depressed, and depression is always anger turned inward."

Empathic Counselor:
"You are feeling bad about yourself right now, and you are filled with shame and anger all at once, I guess."

Client:
"I am just overwhelmed with everything I have to do. There is no way that I will ever get through it."

Intellectualizing Counselor:
"You are stressed out. Stress, however, is an internalized reaction to the external demand that you perceive in your environment. And your internalized reaction can indeed become biochemically triggered."

Empathic Counselor:
"It sounds like you are overloaded and anxious. You don't see any way out."

DEALING WITH THE INTELLECTUALIZING CLIENT

The most effective defense a client has against feelings is intellectualization; it is a great escape to deal with everything at a cognitive level. Clients can talk about feelings and analyze them to death without letting themselves know how they are actually feeling.

The great hazard in intellectualization by the client is that it can so easily draw the counselor into a similar style. Counselors need to work to integrate intellect with feelings. To achieve this, don't confront, but just model empathic acceptance of human feelings and emotions. Consider the following examples:

Intellectualizing client:
"Our marriage fits the description of increased isolation as outlined in existential theory. This is a perfect example of the existential vacuum as described in Frankl's writing." (The client made an important emotional statement, but in intellectual terms.)

Empathic counselor:
"Even though you are married, deep down you feel increasingly lonely." (In this, the counselor acknowledged the feeling the client was trying to talk about.)

Confrontational counselor:
"There you go. You are intellectualizing again. Why don't you tell me how you feel rather than telling me what you think?" (This may be experienced by the client as a direct attack.)

DEALING WITH RELUCTANT/RESISTANT CLIENTS

One of the dilemmas a counselor often faces is how to respond empathically to the client whose verbalization seems primarily resistant or defensive. If you confront and attack the defenses, you punish the few responses and make the client feel inadequate. The more effective way is not to arouse anxiety in the client, but to offer empathic understanding and acceptance without punishing defensiveness. By doing so, you can release your clients from the need to be defensive without punishing them.

How do you do this? You achieve empathic understanding by acknowledging clients' complaints, their efforts, and their aversive circumstances.

The following example illustrates how a counselor uses empathic response to validate client's reactions, however aversive they might be. Note that the counselor not only does not become punitive or take the client's resistance personally, but that she re-frames the client's behaviors into something affirmative.

Client:
"It was very inconvenient for me to come here today, and I'm not feeling very hopeful about coming to therapy."

Counselor:
"You have had some past experiences that cause you to feel not very hopeful about therapy, and yet despite the inconvenience, you had the courtesy to drive here and keep this appointment anyway, didn't you?" (Dolan, 1985, p. 51-52).

EMPATHIZING WITH UNLIKABLE CLIENTS

Some beginning counselors express doubts about their ability to have unconditional positive regard and empathy for clients whom they perceive to be totally unlikable. The story that follows is extracted from a seasoned therapist who responded to a troubled novice with such a concern:

> There's always something to love about a client. Sure it's sometimes hard to find right away but there's always SOMETHING and then the feeling can grow into an acceptance and appreciation of the whole person . . .
>
> . . . Like this guy I saw a week ago. He was unwashed, unkempt, hostile, he smelled bad and I thought, "There's got to be SOMETHING." I sat there looking at him and after a few seconds I noticed that he had only one tooth in his mouth. Only one, but at least he had one tooth. I thought, "This guy has ONE GOOD TOOTH and I can at least appreciate THAT." And then the feelings of appreciation began to spread to the rest of the guy. I found myself wondering about the kind of life he must have had that caused him to become this way, the tragedies and high points of his life, his loves and griefs . . . and pretty soon I felt all the appreciation I needed to feel, with some extra to spare. It's always there if you just let yourself really connect with the person." (Dolan, 1985, p. 46)

If, however, you are working with a client with whom you are unable to be empathic because of personal experiences or values that you have, then you should refer the client to other counselors who do not have this same difficulty. For example, you may be unable to work with a sexual perpetrator because of your aversive reaction to him. In this case you should refer him to another therapist. Another case that some counselors find difficult might be helping a client to work through the decision of whether or not to have an abortion. If the counselor is biased one way or the other about the abortion issue, a referral should be made.

USE OF PAUSE

One of the mistakes beginning counselors make is to ask a question immediately after they have completed a reflection of feelings, advanced empathy, self-disclosure, or immediacy, leaving clients no time to absorb what the counselor has said. This kind of interaction tends to hinder counseling from moving to a deeper level of exploration and discovery of meaning. The urge to escape into probing and questions is usually due to anxiety on the counselor's part to fill in the air.

We recommend that once you have completed your empathic or influencing response, stop. Pause for a moment. Allow the client time to reflect on what you have said, time to process his or her own reaction, and time to decide how he or she will respond to what you just said.

TIMING FOR PACING AND LEADING

Beginning counselors sometimes have difficulty deciding when is the right time to pace and when to lead. As a general rule, strong rapport is a signal that the counselor can lead and move ahead on the client's issues. However, if you are under high stress, it may be a contra-indicator against leading. Research shows that distressed counselors tend to push their clients prematurely (Meier, 1983). Leading a client into change too soon can be dangerous; indeed, as Meier and Davis (1993) warn, "when counselors lead too much they lose their clients, figuratively and literally" (p. 9).

SPEAK BRIEFLY

We have emphasized that counselors need to talk less frequently than do clients. In addition to talking less frequently, beginning counselors often need to learn to be brief and concise in their responses, except when summarizing. A common difficulty that beginning counselors share is being too wordy in their responses. They often deliver too many sentences at one time and have difficulty just stating the major point. As a consequence, their messages are not effectively received by clients. To change, beginning counselors may need to edit what they want to say before speaking. Listen to the audio- or videotape of your practice session. When you spot a wordy response, stop, edit, and then practice the brief alternative response. Try to keep all your responses related to the theme you have identified. Consider the following examples:

Client:
"I really don't think that I want to get involved with Frank again. After we got divorced the first time, I promised myself that I would never go back to a relationship with him because he abused me so badly. I even had a court restraining order against him. But last week he came over to my house and apologized, brought me flowers, and promised to be a husband to me and a good father to our kids. I know I should tell him to go away, but my life is so empty without him."

Counselor's Response #1 (accurate but wordy):
"So you were first married to Frank a number of years ago but he abused you and you even had to get a court restraining order. You feel that you

really should keep him out of your life but he has come back, is treating you nicely, and is promising to be a good father and husband. Although you feel that you should keep him out of your life, you are torn and thinking about getting back with him."

Counselor's Response # 2 (accurate and more concise):
"So although you have ended your relationship with Frank because he was abusive, you are now feeling torn between your longing for love and your desire to keep your resolve to stay away from him."

Client:
"So here is how my day goes. I get up on Saturday and I know I should be going out and having some fun. But, instead I go to the computer and print out a list of all the things that need to be done around the house. I have these things arranged so that I can print them out by how much time they take, how much they cost, or how I have prioritized them in order of need. I determine what I am going to do; then I have a drink and go shopping at the hardware store. I worked until 8:00 at night on Saturday. And then I hate myself for blowing the whole day with work. I usually drink a bottle of gin and think about what a waste my life is."

Counselor's Response # 1 (accurate but wordy):
"So on Saturdays, you get up and consult your computer concerning how you should spend your day. You can choose your project by cost, time, or need. Then you have a drink and go to the hardware store to purchase the needed items. Then you work all day and at night you are angry at yourself for spending the whole day working. Then you drink a bottle of booze and feel bad about yourself." (This counselor is as obsessive as the client.)

Counselor's Response # 2 (accurate and more concise):
"So you don't seem to be able to relax on your days off. You drink to numb the pain."

WHEN IN DOUBT, FOCUS ON FEELINGS

A lot of clients have difficulty recognizing, tolerating, experiencing, expressing or communicating their feelings. They tend to use vague words (such as "upset" "bad" "not too good" "under the weather") to label their emotional experiences. Many clients even feel unentitled to their emotions. They may communicate no emotions at all, keeping their feelings bottled up until they explode. Helping clients identify or focus on their feelings can help them relieve their psychological pain and discover insights into their conditions (Meier & Davis, 1993).

However, many beginning counselors themselves, especially the cognitive type, are not skilled at identifying feelings, either. A counselor's inability to help a client identify feelings usually leads the session to be content-focused or cognition-oriented, without advancing it into a deeper or more meaningful exploration. Therefore, "an ability to recognize . . . feelings in clients is a sign of progress in the beginning counselor" (Meier & Davis, 1993, p. 17).

When you sense that (1) the session is going in circles, (2) the client is lacking progress in personal exploration, (3) you are becoming bored, or (4) you should do something to bring depth to the session, focus on feeling! Take risks; try reflecting clients' feelings or try using advanced empathy (see Chapter 6) to bring feelings into a client's awareness.

EXPECTING HIGHS AND LOWS

It is common for a beginning counselor to be perplexed: in one session the counselor and client productively work toward some deep issues, and the counselor leaves the session feeling like a superstar; in the following session, the client is withdrawn, the session feels likes a drag, and the counselor leaves feeling not cut out for this profession. These kinds of highs and lows are indeed typical when counselors and clients are working on profound—often painful—issues. A client may be afraid to delve too deeply and touch on something too painful. It is normal to want to withdraw for a while. As a counselor, if you can tolerate that feeling of frustration, contain it, and roll with the resistance, then you can expect that you and your client may be riding those highs again in the following session.

COACHING CLIENTS TO USE "I" LANGUAGE

Some clients use "you" language to describe their own experiences. Frequent use of "you" language tends to undermine these clients' abilities to own up to their own experiences. To help clients escape from this kind of "disowning" story-telling habit, the counselor needs to help clients gain an awareness of their use of "you" language and coach them to use "I" language. You can accomplish this in different ways. Consider the following examples:

Client:
"But when you don't have unconditional love at the beginning, you always try to find it or search for it, and always you don't have it, so you keep on searching for it."

Counselor:

"Sometimes it's very confusing for me when you use the word 'you' but actually mean 'I.'"

or

"Say what you just said out loud again. But this time change the word 'you' into 'I.' See how it feels."

CHAPTER SIX

ADVANCED SKILLS:
INFLUENCING SKILLS

In the helping profession, what makes a counselor stand out from others in the crowd is his or her repertoire of advanced skills. Even a layperson can respond with empathic skills (as described in Chapter 3) if he or she has the natural sensitivity to others' emotional experiences. But empathy is not what therapy is all about. Empathy is just the embryo of therapy. To help people really change, it takes more. Clients come to therapy because they have exhausted their resources. Something is not working; something has to be changed. They need more than the empathy and support from a good listener. They need the impetus of therapy. Therapy may be expensive, yet many clients are willing to pay. What makes them willing to pay is that they get from a well-trained therapist something they cannot get elsewhere. That something is the therapist's repertoire of influencing skills. A skilled therapist uses empathic skills to validate the client. But he or she needs to use influencing skills to set a client into change.

Now that we assume that you are familiar with the basic empathic skills and probing skills, you are ready to embark an even steeper road. In this chapter, you will learn the advanced skills, also known as influencing skills. These are the most exciting skills for many beginning counselors who have a real passion for learning and for becoming a professional counselor.

As you work with the client, the road in counseling spirals upward as more advanced skills are needed. You will be challenged when you try to implement the more advanced skills. It takes sensitivity to perform empathic skills (as what you have experienced in learning the skills in Chapter 3); however, it takes insight, courage, and intuition to perform influencing skills. Learning these advanced skills reminds you again of the challenges of learning a foreign language.

The process of counseling goes through stages. After you have paced the client and established a trusting relationship or rapport, the client now should be in a state of receptiveness. The counseling process now moves to the *middle stage (awareness raising stage).* In this middle stage of counseling, the focus changes from what clients are saying toward discovering the underlying patterns of their lives.

Your tasks in the middle stage are: (1) to help clients develop an emotional awareness of ineffective coping patterns, (2) to help clients work through resistance to change, (3) to help clients accept, own up, and honor old patterns, (4) to help clients recognize growth edges, and (5) to help clients envision preferred outcomes.

In this middle stage, you continue to use reflective listening skills, and start to add *influencing/advanced skills.* In influencing skills, the counselor primarily leads the client. Influential skills lead the client's exploration and self-awareness to a deeper level. However, as Dolan (1985) warns, "Each lead should be followed by several instances of additional pacing behavior. This will ensure that rapport is maintained" (p. 69).

Advanced skills discussed in this chapter include:

- Advanced empathy
- Counselor self-disclosure
- Immediacy
- Confrontation: Challenging
- Feedback-giving

All influencing skills share one similarity: they all deal with issues *in a meta-communication level.* In contrast, the basic reflective listening skills (Chapter 3) deal with issues more or less on a content level. What is meta-communication? To answer this question, you need to know that "The therapist-client relationship is complex and multifaceted; different levels of communication occur simultaneously" (Teyber, 1997, p. 16). At least two levels of communication go on in this relationship: content and process. The content level is the overtly spoken material of what is discussed. The process level is the meta-communication level. It goes beyond the content and toward how the therapist and client interact and how the therapist and client communicate. Meta-communication is about the two parties communicating about their communication. This means you as a therapist need to take some risks to go beyond social norms to talk with clients about the interaction between you. To make it work, however, you need to use meta-communication in a sensitive and respectful way, pacing your clients within their comfort levels.

Meta-communication requires complex mental operations. It requires you to recognize the process as well as the *content,* and to realize *the interplay of the many underlying dynamics* in client's problems. As described in the first chapter, learning counseling language is like learning a foreign language: It is both challenging and rewarding; it requires courage, effort, energy, persistence, patience, and intelligence.

In this chapter, we will give you tips on how to learn this foreign language of advanced counseling skills so that you can move the counseling process through the middle stage. To give you an overview, this chapter focuses on the following skills:

- **Helping clients accept, own up, and honor old patterns:** Use immediacy, process self-disclosure, advanced empathy, corrective feedback, and confrontation.
- **Helping clients work through resistance:** Use reflective listening skills, pacing, and self-disclosure.
- **Helping clients recognize growth points:** Use advanced empathy, "unique outcome" questions, and confirmative feedback.
- **Helping clients envision preferred outcomes/goals:** Use reflexive questions.

ADVANCED EMPATHY

Advanced empathy is a deeper level of empathy in which you communicate the meanings and feelings that the client is not yet aware of. It is advanced because you are one step ahead of your client regarding awareness into his or her inner experiences and narratives.

Advanced empathy occurs when you have a deeper insight into the client's struggles. You are crawling even deeper under the skin of the client and are sensing what he or she is experiencing. You point out the client's underlying feelings, recurring themes, and unrecognized resources. In using advanced empathy, you uncover hidden messages and feelings that the client is not fully aware of or is only half saying.

Questions you may ask yourself to deepen your insights as you listen to a client are like these:

- What is the person only half saying?
- What is the person hinting at?
- What is the person saying in a confused way?
- What messages do I hear behind the explicit messages?
- What messages do I hear from the nonverbal behaviors?
- What is the open edge for growth?

Using Advanced Empathy

Advanced empathy may take six forms:

✔Reflecting the implicit emotions

✔Identifying patterns
✔Connecting islands
✔Exploring growth edges
✔Vivid graphic language
✔Successive approximations

These forms are explained in the following sections.

Reflecting the Implicit (Unexpressed) Emotions

The first form of advanced empathy is reflecting clients' implicit or underlying emotions. These emotions have usually not been stated or recognized by clients. Basic empathy (as described in Chapter 3) conveys clients' *explicit or stated emotions,* whereas advanced empathy (described in this chapter) conveys clients' *implicit emotions,* which are usually not talked about, are buried inside, and underlie the explicit behaviors. For example:

What Is Seen (Explicit)	Underlying (Implicit)
belittling behaviors	jealousy
frustrations	inadequacy
anger (men)	hurt or fear
hurt (women)	anger

To reflect the implicit emotions, you need to pay attention to the feelings hidden behind the nonverbal behaviors or expressed messages. Study these examples:

Client:
"I have been thinking about going back to graduate school. Really, it might be good for me so that I can meet more people and network. It will give me something to do in the evening and something to talk about with my friends."

Counselor:
"You are talking about going back to graduate school, yet from *your voice I get a sense that you do not really feel enthusiastic about it* (reflecting unexpressed emotions)."

Client:
"To be honest, I don't really have the confidence to go back to graduate school right now. But I feel guilty about wasting my time in this pointless job."

Client:
"There are other White colleagues with less experience who get a higher salary than I do. I resent the system."

Counselor:
"I hear your resentment loudly (basic empathy). Although you have succeeded in asking for a higher salary, *I get a sense that the feeling of being discriminated against still torments you."* (Italics show the counselor's advanced empathy where the client's covert feeling of being discriminated is made explicit.)

Here are a few more examples. All advanced empathy statements are in italics.

"Although you did not talk much about your feelings, each time we discuss your mother's verbal abuse, you *hang down your head and clench your fist, and I sense strong emotion inside of you."*

"As you spoke about your relationship with your girlfriend, you *chuckled. I sense a feeling of uncertainty in your voice."*

"When you talk about your engagement, *I sense a bit of uncertainty as your voice trails* **off."**

"I get a sense that you tell yourself 'Getting mad is not O.K.'"

"When you are saying that you know your marriage is over, *I sense some hopefulness in your voice* **that might suggest you still think it has a chance."**

"From the tears in your eyes, I sense that you care deeply for **your brother."**

"I hear anger in your voice. You feel like a sucker for being so giving. **On the other hand, you really want to help people make their lives better. It must be frustrating and confusing to feel torn by opposites."**

"You said that you are hurt by your husband's indifference. *I also hear anger in your voice."*

Identifying Patterns

The second form of advanced empathy is identifying patterns. Continued patterns that underlie the client's behaviors are called *themes*. Themes may be (1) a common thread that runs through the sessions, (2) a client's behavior patterns used to cope with the problems, or (3) the consequences caused by these coping patterns. Experienced counselors analyze a client's theme in their minds simultaneously as they actively listen to the client. Beginning counselors usually need to sit down and work out a map after a session to comprehend the themes hidden under a client's dispersed presentation.

Many themes can emerge in counseling sessions. A theme usually has three components: (1) common thread or interaction patterns, (2) coping patterns, and (3) the vicious circle resulting from the coping behaviors. These theme components are explained further in the Theme Analysis section of Chapter 9.

When you recognize the client's pattern, the consequences of the pattern, or a common thread across sessions, it is important that you share it with your client as soon as you sense that the client is ready. Sharing the themes with your client brings insight and focus into counseling. Failing to do so, on the other hand, may prevent clients from becoming aware of their thematic patterns.

Practice theme analysis frequently after your sessions so that you can identify themes easily. Use the following examples to familiarize yourself with the verbal cues counselors give clients to signal when they have identified themes. All italics indicate signals that the counselor is going to identify a theme for the client.

Counselor:
"From the several events you shared, it seems that *you have a pattern of letting other people make decisions for you.*"

Client:
"But once they do, then I'm usually dissatisfied, although I don't let them know."

Counselor:
"Steve, *I have a theory* for your growing anxiety and fatigue. Please tell me whether it fits or not: One, you stretch yourself to work full time at work and part time at school. Two, you feel compelled to compete hard with others. And three, the emotional drain of getting ready for a marriage is enormous for anyone, including you. All these things together are bound to take their physical and emotional toll. You are a strong person, but not a Superman. This inevitably leads to your increased anxiety and fatigue."

Client:
"Now that you say it, it makes sense. The point is that I'm not managing it well."

Following are a few more examples. Please note that many terms in the parenthesis are new for you. Please read the Theme Analysis section of chapter nine for detailed explanations of these terms.

"Your reaction to the loss of your job *seems to be consistent with* your inability to express emotions (common thread/interaction pattern)."

"This tune seems to come up again and again; that is, you often feel responsible for other people's choices (common thread/interaction pattern)."

"Throughout our conversation, it appears to me that you seem to need outside approval to think that your feelings are okay (interaction pattern)."

"I see a pattern here. You seem to avoid communicating your feelings anytime someone upsets you (interaction pattern)."

"So let me tie it all together. You sleep a lot, have trouble getting to move in the morning, lose interest in people, and have not been productive at work. *Sounds like you are drained overall, not just in one area of your life* (common thread across sessions)."

"I see *a pattern in our sessions.* You have a tendency to talk a lot about what you think and glaze over what you feel (interaction pattern). Perhaps this loss of touch with feelings is making your decision-making even more difficult (the vicious circle)."

"Let me share with you *the motif I see in our sessions.* You seem to feel that it's your fault you feel insecure about your relationship with your husband (interaction pattern). And your past experience confirms your feelings that it is you who are to blame when things go wrong (past training)."

"This theme seems to be obvious. You feel disappointed in yourself. And this disappointment in yourself is a direct consequence of your awareness of *other people making decisions for you and your failing to take charge* (interaction pattern)."

"This thread seems to come up again and again, that is, not being assertive in groups (interaction pattern) tyrannizes your feeling about yourself and your relationship with others (circular consequences)."

"This theme seems to run through our sessions. Your separation anxiety (common thread) is having some control over your life. It has controlled the activities you do and your relationship with others (circular consequence)."

"I see a sameness in some of the sessions we have had—a common thread that creeps in. You express concern about others' perceptions about you, about how people think about you. I sense that you are especially stressed out when you worry about how others would perceive you if you did not do things the way they expect you to do."

"It seems that *a pattern that has been happening is that* you are over-compensating in a way that is causing you a lot of anxiety. You

seem to anticipate negative things and then over-prepare yourself to
compensate for it or fix it. Some of this overcompensation seems to
make things better for you, but in another way it is causing you a lot
of tension and leading you to respond to regular challenges in anxiety
ridden patterns."

Connecting Islands

The third form of advanced empathy is connecting islands, also known as *influencing summarization.* To connect islands is to tie together the seemingly irrelevant parts in the client's story and to strike an insightful interpretation. Connecting islands is a more advanced skill than either basic summarization or identifying patterns. In connecting islands, the counselor weaves strands of events that comprise the client's stories. Then the counselor uses a psychodynamic interpretation that provides an insight to help the client tie together different, seemingly unrelated events. Thus *a framework* is developed to help clients understand their problems. Again, connecting islands goes beyond identifying patterns. Because it provides a framework, the skill of connecting islands is also called *influencing summarization,* as compared to basic summarization.

The following are examples of how to connect islands. The italicized parts are the verbal cues that signal counselor attempts to connect client events together to make an interpretation. Clients are usually given a psychodynamic insight as an interpretation of their behaviors.

> *"I see some connection standing out here.* In an earlier session, you mentioned that you feel neglected by your husband. Today you compare your husband to your emotionally unavailable father. The pain of *being neglected by a emotionally unavailable male* (a psychodynamic interpretation) seems to run through your significant relationships."

> *"I see a connection throughout your stories. You* said you started assuming the adult male role of the family in your teenage years because there was no adult male around. You became, literally, your mom's father and your sister's protector. Now, as an adult, because you find there is no one in the neighborhood to fight away the gangs, you feel like you are called to fill in. *The mission of being a rescuer seems to fall on your shoulders when there is a need* (a framework of interpretation)."

> *"I notice a similarity about* the way you reacted to your grandmother's death, your confrontation with your boss, and your reaction to your friend's moving. *In all these situations, you seem to not allow your inner emotions to arise from the events for fear of having to confront the sense* of loss (an interpretation)."

"So you're on bad terms with your father, your boss, and your professor. *The connection I see here seems to be that you have a hard time maintaining relationships with authority figures* (an interpretation)."

"*I see a connection* over our last few sessions. *The unresolved guilt and anger you carried from the relationship with your mother are spilling over into the relationship with your daughter* (an interpretation)."

"Let me check with you to see whether the connection I see fits you or not. The past sessions you mentioned feeling like a little girl when pressed by your *boss.* You feel powerless in that situation. Then when you talked about your *mom,* you seemed to feel powerless because nothing would ever be good enough for her. And now when facing your *sister's* avoidance attitude toward her own illness, you feel powerless for not knowing what to do to help her. *In all these incidents, you revert to feeling like a powerless child dominated by an overbearing figure like your mother* (an interpretation).

Exploring Growth Edges

The fourth form of advanced empathy is exploring clients' growth edges. A growth edge is a painful area of client's life that can be transformed into a growing point. Usually, clients' presenting stories are negative and problem-saturated. If you participate in this kind of "problem talk," clients won't get better, no matter how much insight into their problems they gain. Focusing on the pathology of the client does not lead to therapeutic change. Rather, by focusing on the growing edges (the emerging aspects of the client's experiences), the therapists are more likely to find exceptions from the problem-saturated stories and to co-construct change with clients.

As is typical in Narrative Therapy (Freedman & Combs, 1996; White, 1989), the therapist advances to focus on the *growth edges and the unique outcomes* (White, 1989). This is more than just affirmation. Rather, the therapist goes one step forward to focus on the *resiliency* of the client, on *the exceptions to the problems,* or on what Freedman and Combs (1996) call it, the "Sparkling Events". These are the aspects of client life that shine and illuminate the client's *forgotten strengths and resources.* It is these growth edges that point to potential paths of change.

To master this skill, you may want to practice advanced case conceptualization (Chapter 9) so that you can see the growth edges easily.

The principle in the skill of exploring growth edges is to (1) describe the client's difficulties, and (2) focus on the client's resiliency or any signs of triumph.

The following gives examples of how to connect islands. The italicized parts are the verbal cues that signal counselor attempts to focus on the client's resiliency or any signs of triumph.

Client:

"My father has had Parkinson's disease for the past eight years. I have to take care of my family because my mother died when I was five. I have to do all the work around the house, take care of Dad, and still go to school. It is like I have no life of my own."

Counselor:

"You have carried a tremendous burden of responsibility since you were little. All *these years you have just gritted your teeth and done it."*

Client:

"I'd like to move up in administration at my university, but I am terrified of public speaking. The higher up you go, the more public speaking you need to do."

Counselor:

"Even though the public speaking scares you, *you still long to take up a leadership role and realize your potential."*

Client:

"I feel like I don't want to live anymore. There is nothing to look forward to. I get up depressed and things just get worse as the day goes on."

Counselor:

"You are in a depressed state with little to look forward to, *yet something within you gives you the courage to get up and face each day."*

Client:

"I didn't have that kind of relationship with my parents when I was little, so I find myself searching for it elsewhere and I keep on searching for it. I like this relationship in counseling; although it is professional, it still helps me."

Counselor:

"Even though you are afraid to, you want to speak about how you feel, and you have found that you *can do that here, with me."*

Here are a few more examples:

"You stated that it is hard for you to change and try new ways of acting, yet it seems that *coming to counseling is a step in that direction* **and** *it reflects a lot of courage on your part."*

"*Despite* all that's been put on your shoulders, you *are able to find a way to get it all done well."*

"When everyone else had given up, you *were able to keep your head up and move on."*

"You have come very close to exploring the fear underneath your heroic life style. I know that it would have been much easier to hide behind your shield and not face your fear, *and you have met your fear head on.*"

"You stated that you have difficulty feeling worthy enough to take care of yourself. And it seems that *by discussing this issue* with me in counseling, you *are stepping in the direction of taking control of your life by taking care of yourself.*"

"To get the kind of attention and recognition that you want, you could wait for people to give it to you; *instead, you go and seek it out.*"

"It seems that in facing trials, you always manage *to rise above the obstacles. You never quit!*"

Vivid Graphic Language

The fifth form of advanced empathy is using vivid graphic language. Frequently in counseling, clients imply a lot of feelings in their expressions, but have trouble approaching them directly. Often they feel that their feelings are illegitimate. To help clients experience more fully their marginalized feelings, you have to use language that is specific, that captures the precise nuance (subtlety) of what the client is trying to say. Graphic language comes into use. Graphic language can conjure up the image and bring up the strong emotions behind that image. Graphic language gives clients permission to recognize their feelings more fully.

Example:

Client:
"All she does in the meeting is whine. She never says anything positive. All she does is minimize everything I say."

Counselor A:
"That really drives you crazy (basic empathy)."

Counselor B:
"When she starts that perpetual whining, you feel like standing up and strangling her (advanced empathy: vivid and graphic, pointing out what was implied)."

Here are some more examples. Again the italicized parts indicate counselor's use of vivid graphic language.

"Although you try not to think about the fact that you have cancer, it is there in the back of your mind, like a fear eating away at your peace of mind."

"You say you don't want to talk about this, but it haunts you, *gnawing at your stomach like hunger pains.*"

"Every time your mother verbally abuses you, *you feel that she has sunk a knife in your heart and you want to scream* until she sobs 'I'm sorry!'"

"You said you don't want to speak about it, but inside *you feel like something is ripping, tearing, clawing in your gut, bursting to get out.*"

Successive Approximations

The sixth form of advanced empathy is using successive approximations. This involves starting out with a less strong word and reading the client's reaction to it. If the client's nonverbal feedback gives clues that stronger words would still be within the implied message, then add the stronger words.

Successive approximation is a useful way to get as far ahead of the client as possible without taking over direction.

For example:

Client:
"When my mother died, I was seven years old and I did not know that she had committed suicide. I did not find this out until one of my relatives told me that she had jumped off the roof of a bank building."

Counselor:
"I bet you felt surprised and shocked, even hurt and perhaps shamed and guilty."

Other examples:

"After you connect your current situation with what your father did to you, you are hurt and angry, maybe even devastated."

"It seems that you are angry, maybe even enraged at your boss."

"I guess you feel sad . . . despondent, even."

"You seem hurt by your husband's comment, almost shattered."

"When your husband yells at you, you feel anxious, fearful . . . even afraid for your life."

The Impact of Advanced Empathy From the Client's Point of View

- Clients see patterns in their behaviors.

- Clients begin to understand why they are caught their current pattern of behavior.
- Clients began to see their patterns and emotions with deeper understanding.
- Clients can see areas for their growth despite desperate situations.
- Clients experience more hope as they reach greater self knowledge.

COUNSELOR SELF-DISCLOSURE

The second type of advanced or influencing skill is "counselor self-disclosure." In keeping with the notion of genuineness or transparency, you can use self-disclosure to maintain a genuine relationship with clients. Self-disclosure enables you to encounter the client as a human being. Appropriate counselor self-disclosure (1) provides modeling of openness and risk-taking for clients, and (2) increases clients' trust in the counselor (Yalom, 1983).

Please note that counselor self-disclosure should be distinguished from self-disclosure in social interaction. In social interaction, self-disclosure is expected to be symmetrical; that is, people disclose to each other at about the same pace, proportion, or depth (Garner, 1991). However, in a counseling setting, self-disclosure is conducted economically. Counselor self-disclosure is done only when the disclosure can help the client; as Yalom puts it, "Self-disclosure must be in the service of the primary goal of therapy" (Yalom, 1983, p. 162).

When counselors self-disclose too excessively, it may indicate that the counselor has unfinished business from his or her personal life that may require professional services.

Note: Our clinical experience with minority clients tell us that they prefer counselors who self-disclose. Counselors who disclose their awareness of potential personal biases are more likely to develop trusting relationships with minority clients.

Using Counselor Self-Disclosure

Counselor self-disclosure may involve any of the following:

✔Process self-disclosure: disclosing an immediate, within-the-session experience

✔Personal disclosure: disclosing a meaningful experience or a fact about yourself

✔Professional reassurance: disclosing a reaction to the client's progress

Process Self-Disclosure

The first form of counselor self-disclosure is process self-disclosure. "Process" is the opposite of "content." *Content* refers to the plain, literal topic of the conversation. *Process* refers to (1) the meta-communication, (2) "what the client and counselor are feeling and experiencing at that moment" (Meier & Davis, 1993, p. 13), and (3) the relationships between the two parties.

Process self-disclosure is a skill by which you reveal your *reactions* to client's situations (Meier & Davis, 1993). It conveys a sense of presence and immediacy. The use of process disclosure can "increase clients' experience of their feelings in the here-and-now" (Meier & Davis, 1993, p. 17). The sharing of your *emotional reactions* can model for clients that it is okay to have such feelings (Meier & Davis, 1993).

There can be three types of process self-disclosure:

- Disclosing Emotional Connection

    "As I listen to what happened to you in your childhood, *I'm moved* to tears."

    "As you spoke about your uncle, *I felt angry and sad.* "

    "*I feel saddened* as I hear you speak about your loss."

    "I feel my stomach tighten right now as I hear the way your step-father treated you."

- Disclosing Physical Condition

    "I want to let you know that I *am not feeling that well* today. I had a sinus problem last night and did not sleep well, so if I seem a bit out of sorts, that's why."

    "I was on-call last night—got only two hours of sleep. If I appear fatigued, that is the reason."

    "I just want to let you know that I have a migraine headache today, and if I seem a little different, it is because I am taking medication."

- Disclosing Misunderstanding

    "I think I *really misunderstood you there.* Maybe you could tell me again so that I could try to get it clear."

    "I had a feeling in the last session that we were stuck and that we were not working in synchrony. So I have given a lot of thought to that session and looked over my notes from previous sessions. And *I just realized that I have been missing the boat.*"

"As you may have noticed, I have been feeling lost in grasping some important points you have tried to make. I have reflected on a few things I had overlooked, and I would like to share these ideas with you."

Personal Disclosure

The second form of counselor self-disclosure is personal disclosure. Often clients feel as if their emotions are not normal or legitimate. Counselors can use personal disclosure to normalize the client's feelings. This involves reveal-ing personal experiences *that have happened outside the therapy session. Personal disclosure should never be more than a few sentences.* Personal dis-closure is only done when it is likely to be facilitating to the client.

There can be two types of personal disclosure:

- Personal Disclosure Upon Client's Request

  Client:
  "Are you married?"

  Counselor:
  "Yes, I've been married for two years."

  Client:
  "Have you ever been divorced?"

  Counselor:
  "I honor your desire to know this about me. Maybe you are asking this question because you believe that only divorced people can understand what it is like to be divorced and help people go through that loss. I have never been divorced but I have had many losses in my life."

- Personal Disclosure That Normalizes Client's Feeling

  Client:
  "I don't know how other Hispanic families act, but in my family, we don't express much emotion. I want to be able to express more than what I've had with them, and I'm thinking maybe my first step will be to show my feelings with them so I can move on. But it's so hard to start, and I'm thinking I'll never be able to do it, because it's just so painful, hard."

  Counselor:
  "Yes, it takes pain to change. As a White male in this society, I have been expected to be assertive and to speak what's on my mind, and *I haven't been that way. When I was younger I was very much the*

introvert, I would not initiate. It took me a lot of pain, hard work and practice to get to where I am now."

Other examples of personal disclosure from the counselor:

"When I first moved to America I was 18 years old. I left all my friends and my family to come here. *I remember feeling so lost, alone and isolated."*

"When my friends don't ask me about myself as often as I would like, *I feel lonely, too."*

"I feel the pressure to he competent and strong all the time, too, because I am a therapist. Sometime I yearn for someone to accept my human frailty."

"When I was at your age, *I was also confused* **about not having a clear direction of where to go."**

"I experienced those same emotions **when my father died."**

"I had a very similar experience in my life and *it was painful for me."*

"I, too, lost my father to cancer. *I remember feeling scared, anchorless, and relieved at the same time."*

"When I was in college, I also felt like just another number."

Professional Reassurance

The third type of counselor self-disclosure is professional reassurance. This type of response is similar to the skill of affirmation used in basic empathy, but adds the therapist's gut feelings. Professional reassurance allows the counselor to express how he or she feels about the client's progress. This is usually a positive boost for clients who respect the therapists' opinions of how they are progressing. When done sincerely, it is a high form of positive reinforcement.

"I feel really confident in your ability to take care of yourself."

"I feel excited for **you that you have come to this new level of insight about the pattern in your life."**

"I'm glad for **your accomplishment, which is so much in spite of the difficulties."**

"I'm proud **of all the hard work you did in this session."**

"I'm really proud **of how you owned up to your anger and guilt today."**

"I am really gratified **that you are not defensive in talking about this issue."**

"I am impressed by the fact that you have been able to communicate your anger to your husband and your mother without hurting their feelings."

"It has been striking for me to hear you tell yourself. 'It's time to stop blaming other people and to start taking charge of my own life.'"

"I am glad to see that you have followed your plan for change very well."

"I see how hard you have been trying to use the skills you learned in assertiveness training. *I am very proud of you."*

Skill Differentiation

Be aware of the differences between self-disclosure and immediacy:

"As I listen to you talking about your pregnancy, I notice that you are kicking your legs restlessly." (This is not self-disclosure. Because the counselor did not reveal her/his feelings. This is immediacy, as covered in the next section)

Here is one way to change the response to self-disclosure:

"As I listen to you talking about your pregnancy, *I feel as worried* as you are."

The Impact of Counselor Self-Disclosure From the Client's Point of View

- Clients feel that their distressing feelings are normal.
- Clients feel a human bond with the therapist.
- Clients feel that they are not alone in their existential struggle.
- Clients feel that the therapist cares about them and is willing to show vulnerability.

IMMEDIACY: DIRECT, MUTUAL TALK

The skill of immediacy, or direct mutual communication, is to discuss directly and openly what is happening in the here-and-now. Immediacy deals with what is happening in the relationship between the client and the counselor. This immediacy response enables counselors to focus on the relationship between them and the client in the therapy session. Carkhuff and Pierce (1975) state, "Immediacy is the fullest means of communication available to indicate the degree of lifefulness of a person. If we cannot communicate with immediacy at critical moments, then we have failed to communicate to the helpee (others) the fullness of life"(p. 130).

One reminder: Therapists should not jump in with immediacy without contemplation. As a rule of thumb, before you engage the client with the immediacy talk, you need to wait until you are sure that the observed client interaction or body language is a pattern, that is, an interaction or body language that has happened two or three times, and you have reflected on them.

Using Immediacy

Immediacy is descriptive, with no level of interpretation involved. Two types of immediacy are discussed in this chapter:

✔Non-verbal immediacy
✔"I-You" relationship immediacy

Non-Verbal Immediacy

If a client's certain nonverbal behaviors appear more than twice and you have a hunch that these nonverbal behaviors contain significant meanings or feelings, it is important to share your "process observation" with the client. When you do so, a deeper level of client exploration and self-awareness is more likely to follow.

In general, not all client nonverbal signals convey meanings. It will be perceived as intrusive and offensive if you constantly comment on a client's trivial nonverbal behaviors. In the initial stage of counseling, even when a client's nonverbal behaviors convey significant meanings, these nonverbal cues should be kept in your mind as sources of information and not as subjects for explicit discussion. Clients who receive explicit verbal discussion about their nonverbal cues are likely to feel as if they are treated as an object (Yalom, 1983). To restate the point: Don't use non-verbal immediacy in the initial stage of counseling.

When the working relationship with a client is established, however, sharing process observation (nonverbal observation) may be used as a form of immediacy. Nevertheless, the language used for immediacy needs to be respectful, non-intrusive, and sensitive. When you share a non-verbal observation, simply share what you see in the here-and-now without either interpreting the meaning of the client's nonverbal behavior or confronting the client's discrepancy. In each of the following examples, note how the counselor points out the client's non-verbal signals.

"**Whenever you talk about your father,** *your face lights up.*"

"*Your eyes really sparkle* **whenever you talk about your grandmother.**"

"**I'm aware that** *you are wringing your hands right now.*"

"**As you say that,** *you are giggling.*"

"*I notice a facial tic in your cheek* **when we talk about your questioning of being a token of affirmative action at your work.**"

"**When you said that,** *you literally pulled yourself back* **as if you were hit in the chest by what your wife said.**"

"**I notice that as you speak about this** *your face tightens.*"

"**I notice that when you talk about painful events,** *you laugh.*"

"**I notice that when you say this, you** *have fear in your eyes.*"

"**I realize that whenever you talk about your father,** *you begin to fidget nervously.*"

"**When you speak of the serious situation of possibly losing your job,** *there is laughter in your voice.* **I wonder whether you notice it or not?**"

"**I notice that when you speak of your relationship with your step-father,** *you begin tapping your foot very quickly.*"

"**As you talk about your brother,** *you begin leaning forward.*"

"**I see the pain in your eyes.** *Your tears are walled up when you talked about this.*"

"I-You" Relationship Immediacy

The nature of the therapist-client relationship is the most important tool you have to influence client change (Teyber, 1997). If you recognize that your work with a client is stuck even when you have been empathic and have tried to help him or her gain insight, chances are there are some immediacy issues that need to be addressed. In this case, you can use "I-you" relationship immediacy to open a door toward discussing problems in the working relationship with the client. This kind of "I-you" immediacy puts the client-counselor relationship on the table as a topic for discussion. This type of relationship talk can be a threatening and unfamiliar way of communication for both clients and therapists. Therefore it is important to use sensitive and respectful language.

To apply immediacy, you need to call for a disengagement for a moment from the give-and-take of the current interaction and then process what is happening in the relationship. When it is done sensitively, the "I-you" relationship immediacy talk enables both parties to work through the impasses and bring closeness and progression to the therapeutic interaction. This "I-you" relationship immediacy talk, however, entails assertiveness on the counselor's part. As Egan (1976) states, "perhaps more than any of the other interpersonal communication skills, immediacy requires 'guts'—courage or assertiveness"(p. 203).

Note the place in the examples where the counselor brings out aspects of the client-counselor relationship issue.

Client (a young man longing for independence and having difficulty achieving his goal):
"I really don't have much to talk about today. (Pauses and glances out the window.) Not much happened this week. I chatted with my mother about finding a place of my own. (Glances out the window.) We had a long talk. (Sips on coffee.) It was a good talk." (Fidgets and looks down at the floor.)

Counselor:
"From the way you move, I get the feeling that *you are having difficulty telling me* what occurred."

Client (a middle-aged divorced woman who finds herself in the presence of a young male counselor):
"I feel a little nervous about discussing my problem with you. How much do you know about women and marriage? Is there any female counselor available?"

Counselor:
"Because I am a unmarried young man, *you are wondering whether or not I can understand your problems and have enough experience to be able to help you.*"

Client (an emotionally needy client):
"I did all the things you suggested last week to reach out to people, and it worked out pretty well. But I still feel lonely, and I need you to tell me what to do about it."

Counselor:
"It seems that you are asking me to tell you what to do, which will produce the same problem for us in therapy that you are having at home with your mother. So, instead of having me tell you what to do, let's look into what is going on for you when you face a problematic situation."

Client (Having spent the first ten minutes of the session whining about trivialities):
"It has been a very boring week. All the same stuff. It's pretty cold today so I wore this really heavy jacket. And now I am really too hot. Have you

changed the painting on the wall? I have a shirt very much like the one you have on."

Counselor:
"As I listen to you, I find myself wondering *why we are not talking at a deeper level as we usually do."*

Other examples:

"Could we stop for a moment? We started out today with you seeming upbeat and relaxed. Then we started talking about your starting college. Since then *our conversation has been strained. I'm wondering whether something has happened between us to cause this breakdown in our communication or you are just concerned about starting college."*

"I am feeling that I've lost you right now **and that I am not able to see the meaning your story holds for you. Can we stop for a moment and look at what is going on here?"**

"When you talk about these pains, you start laughing. You told me that you use your comic persona to deal with others when in pain, to cover your vulnerability. *And you do that with me here in the session, too."*

"You have just stood up for yourself by disagreeing strongly with me. I am wondering what you think or if you are afraid how I might respond."

"I'm concerned that *you are seeing me as your problem solver."*

"You seem a bit uneasy today, and frankly, I feel the same. **Let's process what causes this feeling."**

"Mary, I'm sensing some tension *between us,* **and am wondering what led to it."**

"I am sorry. *I don't feel comfortable meeting you socially* **outside of therapy."**

"I wonder *how this power struggle with your husband you have been talking about may also get going between you and me here in the session. Where do you see the control issue in our relationship?"*

The following examples combine "I-you" immediacy with interpretation.

"You are hesitant to open up to me because you had opened yourself up in the past with other people but were left alone to deal with all the pain that accompanied it, and you are afraid that if you open up to me this time, I might do the same thing, leaving you feeling injured all over again."

"I understand that one part of you wants to trust me and that another part of you doesn't feel safe at all. You had taken risks to trust others in the past but were taken advantage of, leaving you feeling hopeless and depressed. I understand how much it would hurt you if I betray your trust, and I do not want you to go through that terrible experience again."

"In the jail you have learned to never let your guard down, to give no chance of being exploited. Even right now, you are not sure whether you can trust me with your feelings or whether I'll use them to exploit you."

"You have felt that everybody is on your back wanting you to be more committed in their area of interest. Right now I wonder if you see me as another one of those people on your back making demands for your time."

Suggestions for Counselors in Using Immediacy

- Use immediacy skills only when you have developed trust with your client. Timing matters! If used prematurely, clients may feel threatened.
- Identify your feelings that are evoked by the client's patterns of communication. Your feelings usually can tell you what is going on in the relationship.
- Identify your feelings that are associated with your bodily reactions to the client's message. Your body is very sensitive to what is going on between you and your client. Listen to your body.
- Focus not only on what is being said, but also on what is not being said. What is not said sometimes speaks louder about the relationship than words do.
- Observe the nonverbal.
- Respond in the present tense.
- Express yourself moderately and sensitively.
- Be ready to follow up openly and non-defensively.

Nonverbal Cues in Here-and-Now Observation

As a rule of thumb, a client's nonverbal cues do not convey messages all by themselves; rather, they should be considered together with the verbal context a client is sending or receiving. Body language speaks louder than the spoken words because most people cannot consciously control their non-verbal cues for an extended period of time. Thus, non-verbals cues can give therapists insights into what clients are experiencing at the moment. Garner (1991) suggests that a client's face conveys the emotion or lack of emotion he or she is experiencing, whereas the rest of the body reveals the intensity of that emotion. In other words, you may read whether clients are sad, angry, depressed, anxious, and so on, from their faces; but how intense those specific emotions are may be revealed in the body. Beginning therapists should take time and patience to observe and discern the possible emotions associated with non-verbal cues.

The following are examples for you to practice:

Facial expression:

> tears in the eyes
> dilated pupils
> raised eye brows
> corners of mouth turned down
> a tight jaw
> a stiff upper lip
> lip pursed
> biting of lips
> color in face changed
> tics in the face
> frequent blinking of eyes
> not blinking the eyes
> not looking you in the eye
> wincing of face

Bodily expression:

> pulling the ear
> biting fingernails
> fist tightened
> legs kicking
> body shaking
> finger strangling
> broken voice
> fidgeting
> body turned away
> body slumped
> shoulders dropped
> arms crossed in front of chest

Also, pay attention to nonverbal language that links with *positive emotions:*

eyes sparkling
face lit up
stronger voice projected
smiling
body leaning forward
sitting straight
open body posture

Note: Some of the nonverbal behaviors in the non-Caucasian cultures may convey very different messages. For example, avoidance of eye contact may be a sign of respect or deference for Asians, especially the Japanese (Sue, 1990). Without this knowledge, a well-intentioned beginning counselor may misread a Japanese client's lack of eye contact as inattentiveness, rudeness, or low intelligence. This kind of misinterpretation is perilous for Asian clients.

The Impact of Immediacy From the Client's Point of View

- Clients, for the first time, are aware of how their anxiety is associated with the topics they are discussing.
- Clients are surprised to discover their avoidance behaviors.
- Clients become aware of how others experience them in a relationship.
- Clients are increasingly aware of how their behaviors have influenced their impasses with others.
- Clients are relieved that finally they can learn to deal with their difficulties in the here-and-now interaction with the therapist.
- Clients can learn more constructive ways of functioning in their relationships with others through the new level of honesty and intimacy they experience with the therapist.

CONFRONTATION: CHALLENGING

In counseling, confrontation is a high-level influencing skill used by counselors to draw a client's attention to his or her behaviors that are self-defeating, evasive, unrealistic or defensive. Like other advanced (influencing) skills, confrontation increases a client's awareness of his or her behaviors and the consequences of those behaviors. In sum, confrontation serves to invite the client to examine more carefully his or her interpersonal style and its consequences.

Confrontation should be tentative, non-judgmental, loving, and encouraging. It should be used with good timing. You do not have a right to confront your clients until you have earned their trust.

Confrontation should be based on the counselor's effective listening and careful observation of the client's behaviors. After a confrontation is made, the counselor should use empathic listening skills to facilitate client change. We can't stress enough that confrontation can only be used after you have established a good working relationship with a client.

Beginning counselors usually find it difficult to confront. Meier and Davis (1993) provides a guideline: "A good rule of thumb is that you can confront as much as you've supported" (p. 12).

Using Confrontation

There are three principles of confrontation:

- Describe the client's maladaptive *behavior.*
- Describe *the impact* of such unproductive behavior.
- Use "I" *statements* if possible.

Note: When working with minority clients, avoid using confrontation.

Four types of confrontation are frequently used in counseling:

✔Experiential confrontation:
  – Discrepancy Confrontation
  – Distortion Confrontation
✔Confrontation of strengths
✔Urging to act
✔Information confrontation

All four are discussed in the following sections.

Experiential Confrontation

Experiential confrontation involves telling clients how you experience them differently from the way they experience themselves. At its best, experiential confrontation can help a client break out of self-defeating views of self, of others, and of interpersonal living.

Experiential confrontation has two forms: (1) discrepancy confrontation, and (2) distortion confrontation.

● Discrepancy Confrontation

With discrepancy confrontation, you confront the discrepancy between the verbal and the nonverbal or the verbal and the actual behaviors. In the following examples, italics show how the counselor points out a discrepancy to the client.

"Although you are talking about having resentment for being a victim of prejudices in your job, *I see no emotion showing in your voice and face.*"

"Each time we discuss your mother's verbal abuse, you say it doesn't matter, *but you hang down your head and clench your fist.*"

"I sense something here. You *seem angry with me for being late, but you say that you feel fine.*"

"Even though *you say 'yes' with your words, I see 'no' in your body language.*"

"Although you say you are interested in developing a better relationship with your wife, *I notice that you don't take time to listen to her feelings and to communicate basic understanding to her.*"

"You say that you want to improve your grades, *but I don't see you put much effort and time into reading, library research, and homework.*"

"You say that you agree, *but your tone of voice and scrunched-up face make me believe otherwise.*"

"You are telling me that it really pisses you off, *yet I find you giggled as you said it.* How do you put these two together?"

"You talk about speaking up and being assertive, *but I don't hear a lot of enthusiasm.*"

"You say you want to have a closer relationship with your family, *but I don't hear you put much effort into becoming more intimate.*"

"You say you are calm right now, *but I see you jiggling your leg nervously.*"

"You have come all the way down here to talk to me about this, *but I haven't been convinced that you have a real concern.* Is that all?"

"You're furious because you were exploited and your interests were not taken into consideration, *and yet you let him get away with it.*"

Exceptions for Discrepancy Confrontation

Facial expression, movement, and eye contact are all culturally conditioned kinetics. Before confronting discrepancy, decide whether it is culturally appropriate or not. For Asian clients, restraint of feelings is a culturally sanctioned behavior. These clients may talk about painful experiences with blank facial expressions. A Japanese client may feel extremely uncomfortable, yet he smiles and laughs. When you face this kind of culturally conditioned discrepancy, it is better to avoid confrontation; instead, use advanced empathy (Chapter 6).

For example, with a minority client who is smiling and laughing while talking about her inability to speak up in the staff meeting, a counselor might respond as follows:

Counselor:

"While listening to your difficulty in speaking up, I notice you are smiling and laughing. I get the feeling that it must be very painful to live with this sense of inadequacy."

In this advanced empathy, the nonverbal cues are acknowledged, the feelings underlying that nonverbal cues are reflected, but the culturally conditioned discrepancy is not challenged.

- Distortion Confrontation

The second form of experiential confrontation is distortion confrontation. This involves telling clients that the ways they perceive the situations are distorted or inaccurate views of the events. Often clients misinterpret the actions of others because all people view events through the lens of past experience. Counselors using distortion confrontation provide a reality check for clients.

"You are afraid of teachers due to past experiences. Now you see your teacher as distant, although in reality she is a warm, caring person."

"You say that your boyfriend is insensitive, egocentric, and cold. Yet, by the things you listed that he is doing for you, he seems to be a supportive, caring, and loving person."

"We have talked about your trouble in relating to male authority figures and your desire to relate to them more realistically. Yet, I notice that now you put your supervisor on a pedestal and write him off when he makes mistakes."

"You told me that your dad never pays attention to you. However, he has attended every one of your baseball games this season."

Confrontation of Strengths

The second type of confrontation is confrontation of strengths. This involves pointing out to the client the strengths and resources that he or she has not used or does not use fully.

Client (who described herself as fragmented and cannot tolerate her own emotionality):
"Somehow I feel I shouldn't have revealed myself to you the way I did."

Counselor:
"Well, you seemed able to hold yourself together when the topics were intense."

Other examples:

"You worry that you can't get your life together, but I see you as a resilient and resourceful person. Is there anyone you can remember who also saw these qualities in you?"

"You say you can't, but judging from what you have done, I believe you have the strength to make it this time again."

"You say you are no good to anyone. But I see a kind, caring, helpful person in you. Do others also see you this way?"

"You say that you are concerned about *not having the ability to* complete graduate school, yet you graduated with honors as an undergraduate, and I see you as a motivated, intelligent individual. Do others see you as I do, too?"

Urging to Act

The third type of confrontation is urging clients to act. Many clients talk and talk about taking charge of their lives without ever coming to action. Urging clients to act is to confront them to act in accordance with their best interests, to initiate in life, and to have an impact on others, rather than letting others control the world around them. Be cautious; avoid giving advice or lecturing when you urge clients to act.

"We have discussed your difficulty with going out to meet people due to your introversion. You have gained a great deal of insight through our discussion. *Now the time is right to go out there and test it out.*"

"You say you want to prove your parents wrong. *Now this is a great opportunity to get a good score to prove them wrong.*"

"You sound convinced of what you need to do, *the only thing left is for you to actually try it out.*"

Information Confrontation

The last type of confrontation is information confrontation. This involves giving clients information that they don't seem to grasp fully or that they try to ignore.

Client:
"Maybe I have an eating problem. Yes, since my Mom died, I have used food."

Counselor:
"Food, caffeine, and nicotine **usually work very well to suppress grief."**

Other examples:

"Eleven percent **of teenagers who get AIDS get it from heterosexual relationships."**

"You are afraid to fly because you think every plane will crash, yet statistics show that less than *two percent* **of flights crash per year."**

"You seem to think that you are immune to the need for protection during sex. *This brochure will help explain that there is no 'grace period' for age or number of unprotected encounters."*

"You say you are not smart enough, but you actually got *a higher score than the average* **on the last exam."**

"The college you just mentioned requires *an ACT score of 28 or higher.* **The score you told me you received is not above twenty-eight."**

Skill Differentiation

Be aware of the difference between immediacy and confrontation:

- **Immediacy** does nothing more than only describe behaviors in the counseling session.
- **Confrontation** not only describes behaviors but also points out verbal-body incongruity and perception-reality incongruity.

Consider the following examples that point out the differences:

"You have talked about wanting to get more in touch with your feelings. Yet I notice that every time you get close to your feelings, you run away."
(This is a confrontation. The counselor points out the client's discrepancy between what she says and what she does.)

"I see you push back the moisture in your eyes when you talk about painful feelings."
(This is immediacy. The counselor simply shares her/his observation of the client's nonverbal behavior without pointing out the discrepancy.)

"You say that you have a great relationship with your father. Yet I notice that whenever you talk about your father, you have a tic in your face and you fidget."
(This is confrontation.)

"I see your face tics and your hands fidget whenever you talk about your father."

(This is immediacy.)

Using Confrontation With Care

Remember that confrontation is a high-level influencing skill, and you must exercise caution to ensure you are using it correctly. Good timing and appropriate language are the key. You cannot confront until you have developed trust with your client. The way you confront should be caring, and not offensive. Compare the following:

"Do you always judge all the things you do by such a high standard?"

This is a criticism disguised in question form. This is not confrontation. Confrontation specifies maladaptive behaviors and the impacts of those behaviors. An alternative response may be:

> **"Correct me if I am wrong. I sense that you set pretty high standards for most of the things that you do and you feel defeated when you fail to meet the expectations. Is that right?"**

"Do you always compare yourself with other people?"

This is again a disguised criticism, not an effective confrontation. An alternative response may be:

> **"It seems that you readily compare yourself with other people and put yourself down when you do not measure up. Is that how you experience it?"**

The Impact of Confrontation From the Client's Point of View

- Clients learn to see their behaviors as others do, but in an empathic supportive environment.
- Clients become aware, without feeling attacked, of unrealistic goals and of discrepancies in their thinking.
- Clients become aware of their excuses and self-defeating behaviors while feeling supported in developing more constructive behaviors.
- Clients are invited to examine their interpersonal styles and learn ways to reach real intimacy.
- Clients experience dissonance when their behaviors are viewed from a different perspective. This tends to move them to take a different approach to life.

FEEDBACK-GIVING

The counseling process, when done well, gives clients new awareness of their interaction styles with other people. Many clients are never cognizant of how their behaviors affect other people. In fact, this is probably the greatest cause of many problems that clients have. To help clients increase their awareness in this area, you, as a counselor, need to tell them how they affect you over time. That is, tell the client your inner reaction to her patterns. This skill is called *feedback-giving,* one of the most influential skills a counselor uses to increase a client's awareness.

Using Feedback

Giving clients feedback means giving clients your reaction to their recurring maladaptive interpersonal behavior. This type of feedback-giving is corrective because it tends to bring self-awareness to clients. It tends to help clients realize how their behaviors impact others. Beginning counselors often find this type of feedback-giving threatening as it is immensely different from everyday conversation. Counselors must think of feedback-giving as one of the "asocial" aspects of therapy.

There are many "asocial" aspects of therapy. First, according to Kiesler and Van Denburg (1993), in your clients' daily interactions with people, it is unusual that others will listen carefully to whatever they have to say, because listeners are in a hurry to interrupt with their own views or agendas. In therapy, however, you listen with a concentrated stance. The concentrated listening stance is what makes therapy asocial. Second, during the heat of conversation it is unusual for listeners to carefully track clients' nonverbal messages to detect the concomitant personal implications of their stories. And it is truly a surprising human event when others give feedback on the important positive and negative emotions your clients have induced in them. In therapy, however, you do all of these. This interpersonal feedback that is so asocial actually marks the power of therapy.

Kiesler and Van Denburg (1993) state: "The most essential intervention in interpersonal communication therapy occurs when therapists provide metacommunicative feedback that labels the interpersonal impacts they thematically experience" (p. 5). Feedback-giving is labeling the interpersonal impacts that you experience with your clients. When you notice two cues emerging in the therapy, it is an indication that you need to communicate the interpersonal impact that the clients are having on you. These cues are: (1) your reaction to the client has a repetitive pattern; and (2) the pattern of the client's transactions with you seems parallel to reactions with significant others outside of therapy (Kiesler & Van Denburg, 1993).

When both of these cues happen, you must disengage from these inner reactions induced by your clients and talk directly to them about the reactions transpiring between you. Most centrally, this direct feedback must be provided in a manner that is both confrontative as well as supportive and protective of the client's self-esteem.

We cannot emphasize enough that feedback should be given judiciously. The following are important principles:

- Give feedback *only* when the client is ready and when trust has been developed. The counselor might ask whether the client would like some reactions.
- When giving feedback, *describe the behavior pattern* before giving your reaction.
- Give feedback in the form of describing your reactions to consistent behavior rather than judging the person.

Now, try to differentiate the two:

Judging:
"I don't like you because you are constantly interrupting me."

Describing:
"I have a reaction to the way our conversation goes. You have a tendency to jump in before I finish what I have to say. I often find myself feeling distressed and compelled to talk faster and faster, trying to finish my sentences before you cut me short."

- Give feedback only about things the client has the capacity to change.
- Give feedback in small amounts so that a client can experience the full impact of the feedback. Too much feedback at one time may overload the client and create confusion and resentment.
- Although feedback focuses on recurring behavior patterns, feedback should be a response to a current behavior, not unfinished business from the past. When you notice a client's pattern, make a mental note to yourself. Then give feedback immediately when the pattern reappears again.
- After giving a client feedback, ask the client for reactions to your feedback.

Read the following examples of feedback carefully:

"While listening to you I had some reactions." (Pause.) "We have been talking about your problems in getting along with people. While we were talking, I noticed that you have a tendency to dismiss almost everything I say. I am feeling increasingly frustrated with

your rebuttal. I feel increasingly guarded in talking to you." (Pause.) "Do you think my reaction might tell something about your difficulty in getting along with others?"

"I have some reactions that I would like to share with you. Throughout our sessions, you have rebuffed almost every perspective that I tried to offer. I feel increasingly rejected by you. You say constantly that people in your program discriminate against you. I wonder if they might feel the same way as I do. I wonder if the very way you rebut people may push people away from you."

"We have been working together for a few sessions now. I am feeling increasingly concerned that you are telling me what you think I like to hear rather than working on what is most important for you. I wonder whether you do this in other relationships as well. I wonder whether you tend to put other people's needs or demands first, sacrificing your own best interest."

"I'd like to pause here so that I can tell you what I'm experiencing. As our session has progressed, I have become more and more aware that your voice today has had a whining tone. I am confused about what you really want to say."

"I have some reactions that I'd like to share with you. While we were talking, it seems to me that you keep asking me for help and, when it is offered, you keep saying 'Yes, but . . .' I get frustrated with you when you do that. Do you think my reaction might tell something about why people tend to keep distant from you?"

"I'd like to stop here and give my reactions to what you have been saying. When you talked about the death of your father, I feel a wave of sadness pass through my body, yet I am frustrated because I don't see the same sadness in you. Do you sometimes come across to others as being nonfeeling?"

The Impact of Feedback-Giving From the Client's Point of View

- Clients become aware of how their specific interpersonal styles are carried into the counseling session.
- Clients are able to transfer the knowledge of how they affect the therapist to how they affect others in the outside world.

CHAPTER SEVEN

INTERVENTION TECHNIQUES

W hat is the difference between "counseling skills" and "intervention techniques"? Counseling skills are generic to most forms of counseling and therapy, whereas intervention techniques are specific change agents developed by certain theoretical orientations. Intervention techniques differ from generic talk therapy in that they generally require the clients to engage in certain actions during the session. These actions are done within the session; their purpose is to impel the clients to change. For example, from the perspective of Gestalt therapy, change will occur when clients gain insight into the problem by understanding that they are using only parts of themselves rather than using the integrated whole.

Counseling progresses through stages. If you have applied the basic and advanced skills properly the counseling process should now progress naturally to the Later Stage (or problem resolution stage). In this working stage, counselors use intervention techniques drawn from different theoretical approaches to help clients achieve their preferred outcomes.

This chapter provides some examples of intervention techniques. These include:

- Directives
- Parts dialogue
- "Empty Chair" dialogue
- Reflexive questions
- Narrative steps
- The body awareness technique
- The "Yes" set
- The "No" set

The list here is not meant to be exhaustive. It is imperative that you expand your repertoire of intervention techniques through continued education and personal pursuit. As you develop more experience, you will want to learn about different therapeutic approaches that may help individual clients. As a professional counselor, it is important to take an eclectic approach to counseling, developing new techniques from various counseling frameworks. New approaches can be learned through workshops, experiential learning, consultation, supervision, and personal therapy.

DIRECTIVES

From a Gestalt therapy perspective, clients' problems are perpetuated at times due to their inability to integrate their feelings and needs. Disowning and disallowing are critical mechanisms that maintain people's suffering (Greenberg, Rice, and Elliott, 1993). To help clients integrate the feelings that they feel unentitled to have, it is helpful to use various directives.

Directives are powerful intervention techniques with clients when used appropriately. They should not be equated with commands. Commands expect the person to follow the "shoulds," whereas directives give room for personal decision and the client is free to accept or reject. A directive is a respectful suggestion, yet more powerful than suggestion itself. Remember that the tone of voice also influences the difference between a directive and a command.

Some beginning counselors tend to give directives in the form of a question. Although a question often softens the directive, it is less vibrant and has less impact. Directives need to be given in an assertive and respectful manner.

Using Directives

Four forms of directives are:

✔ Attention Suggestions
✔ Experiential Teaching
✔ Awareness Homework
✔ Paradox

Attention Suggestions (Experiential Focusing)

Attention suggestions direct the client to pay attention to current experience (such as breathing, hidden feelings, non-verbal cues):

> **"Turn your attention inward and see what comes to you."** (Greenberg, Rice, and Elliott, 1993, p. 128)

> **"Take some time to hear what you just said. Don't move on, just stay with it for a while."** (Daldrup, Beutler, Engle, and Greenberg, 1988, p. 60)

Other examples:

> **"OK, see whether you can stay with the sad feeling a bit longer."**
>
> **"All right, try to see whether you can notice your breathing pattern as you tell me this."**
>
> **"As you speak, pay attention to your animated hand gestures."**
>
> **"OK—stay with that angry feeling and talk about how if feels to you."**
>
> **"As you talk about your father, pay attention to your clenched fists."**
>
> **"As you speak, notice how you clench your fists and how your breathing begins to speed up."**
>
> **"As you are talking, try to pay attention to the sadness in your voice."**
>
> **"Listen to the quiver in your voice as you speak."**

Experiential Teaching

Experiential teaching is to teach the client the rationale and the methods required to integrate the "parts" of themselves that they have disowned and that create inner conflicts. In Gestalt therapy, a great deal of attention is paid to different internalized parts within each of us. For example, a Gestaltist, interpreting a dream, would see each object in the dream as a part of the dreamer. The goal of Gestalt therapy is to integrate the parts of a person into a whole. Since the whole is greater than the parts, the person is able to act with fewer inner conflicts and with greater energy. This integration creates stronger people who can experience themselves more fully. Consider the following examples:

> **"It sounds like you are experiencing a kind of argument between two different parts of you. The purpose of putting the two parts in different chairs is to bring this inner dialogue out into the open."** (Greenberg, Rice, and Elliott, 1993, p. 131) (This gives the rationale and the meaning for the two-chair exercise.)
>
> **"OK', I am going to suggest that we put two sides of your struggles in different chairs. Presumably you have never bounced around in chairs before and there may be some self-consciousness about it, but let's just set it up and see where we go, OK?"** (Greenberg et al., 1993, p. 128)
>
> ***"Will you change chairs and tell her how you react to her criticisms?"*** (Greenberg et al., 1993, p. 129)
>
> **"The next thing is** *take a minute and ask yourself,* **'What is this feeling all about?'"** (Greenberg, et al., 1993, p. 129)

"Next time when you feel lonely again, instead of using food to stuff down the feeling of loneliness, befriend it and talk with it. Listen to it as if it is a messenger visiting you to reveal something soulful to you. Say: 'Welcome, my old friend, loneliness! What are you trying to tell me this time?'"

"OK, shift to the chair with the doll, hold the doll, and ask your child within what she felt about it when that happened."

"Ask her if it reminds her of anything that happened to you as a little girl."

"Give your little boy a voice right now and try to talk to your father and express your revulsion."

"Tell the little girl inside yourself, 'It was not your fault. It was not your fault that Daddy did what he did.' Tell her from a place of adult conviction and power."

"Now, put your Adult self there and let your child speak to her."

"Let yourself feel the sadness. Make it okay to cry. Go all the way to the bottom."

"Why don't you talk to this stuffed animal as if it were your friend Peter?"

"Take your time and just decide whether or not you are willing to try that out, and see how it sounds if you say it directly to her."

"Let's take these two conflicting sides of your argument and put one in each one of these empty chairs. Then, I'd like for you to argue each side while sitting in each chair. It may feel a little awkward, but let's just try it and see what we come up with."

"Let's take those sad feelings and mad feelings, put them in each of these chairs and have them talk to each other, and see what comes of it."

"Let's see if we can role play, with you playing both your mom and yourself."

"Because you like to draw, I'd like you to make a picture of your feelings on this piece of paper. Try to draw what your struggles and your anxiety would look like."

"Talk to me as if I were your boss, then tell me how you feel when you get it off your chest."

"I'd like for you to repeat your account of your experience, this time focusing on your strengths throughout the ordeal."

"Now I would like you to get up and shake off what you first felt."

Awareness Homework

Awareness homework is a method or therapeutic action you suggest for a client to carry out outside the session during the week:

> **"During the week, it might be useful for you to write down what you are doing to yourself when you become depressed."**

> **"Here is a little assignment for this week: Whenever you get that scared feeling, write down what's going on so you can be more clear about it."**

> **"This week, I'd like for you to pay attention to some of the external events you are preoccupied with directly prior to your panic attacks."**

> **"I'd like you to go home this week and really be aware of the negative statements that you make about your mother-in-law."**

> **"During this week, I'd like you to pay attention to the social contacts leading up to your binging."**

> **"During this week, you may want to work on the letter writing exercise where you write down your feelings. You don't send the letters. Just keep them. You can decide whether you would like to share them with me next week, to tell me about them, or not to mention them at all."**

Paradox

Paradox is a directive that asks the client to do something that seems to contradict the common notion or belief of what is expected to be done in the therapeutic setting. This is not just reverse psychology. Rather, in the paradox, the therapist prescribes a negative or symptomatic behavior pattern for the client to carry out and secretly wishes the clients to rebel. Thus, the paradox surprisingly brings out a more constructive possibility.

> **"I have an idea. Let's have a debate. I will argue that you don't really have a problem and don't need to change. And I'd like you to argue the other side, that you do have a problem and do need to change. So, I am going to be you, and your job is to convince me that there really is a problem here. OK?"**

> **"It is clear that you are worrying about the problem all the time. I would like you to consolidate your worry time. So every day from 8:00 to 8:30 am, I would like you to sit alone and do nothing but worry about this problem. During the day if you start to worry, make a note about what you are worrying about so that you will have it at**

8:30 am the next day. Make sure that you have worried about the whole problem."

"Because you cannot decide whether you want to commit to your girl-friend or not, I would like you to postpone making the decision as long as you can."

"I am concerned here that you are changing too quickly. So try to slow down your progress."

The Impact of Directives From the Client's Point of View

- Clients focus on actions that will lead to positive change.
- Clients learn experientially rather than intellectually.
- Clients learn methods that they can transfer to similar situations.
- Clients become more empowered in trying new actions rather than being stuck in old patterns.
- Sessions become more alive and more energetic.
- Clients participate intensely in the therapy.

PARTS DIALOGUE: DEALING WITH SPLITS AND INTROJECTION

There are many ways that incomplete experiences can fragment a person. These fragmented experiences are called *splits* or *parts,* such as the part of self that is angry and the other part that condemns anger. Splits stem from *introjections,* which are beliefs internalized whole-heartedly from significant others without evaluation and discrimination. Common introjections held in by many of us may be "Real men don't cry," or "Good girls don't get angry." In a clinical case, the part of self within a client that condemns anger may stem from parental rule against feelings or from parental denial of feelings.

If splits are not integrated into the client's consciousness, the self will be in constant inner conflict, causing unexplainable anxiety and incongruent behaviors. These inner conflicts brew into rifts that are damaging to interpersonal relationships. People may get caught in similar destructive relationships repetitively without understanding the reason.

Using Parts Dialogue

When a client's splits or introjections are observed, the counselor can use *split dialogue* or *introjection dialogue* intervention techniques to facilitate integration. When the two extremes or splits are put into contact, the client usually becomes more aware of the dichotomy in their inner experiences. The awareness gives the client opportunity to negotiate between the two, arriving at some integration.

Counselor:

"Feel the struggle in yourself between the part of you that flushes with anger and the part of you that follows your father's rules."

Client:

"That's exactly it—I feel pulled in both directions."

Counselor:

"*OK.* Excuse your father from the chair for a moment. I'm going to ask you to change the experiment. Would you speak from each of those parts of yourself to the other part? (set up two facing chairs) **Start either place."** (Daldrup et al., 1988, p. 124)

Other examples:

"Now, let the child within you have a voice and say something back to the adult part of *you.*"

"You are talking about two parts of yourself, the responsible Joe and the wandering Joe. The responsible part of Joe wants to settle down and give your fiancée a sense of security, and the wandering part of Joe just wants to keep having affairs. Make the responsible part of Joe talk to the wandering part of Joe about this problem."

"I am going to put another chair beside you. When you hear the voice of fear, talk from the chair where you are sitting. When you hear the voice of self assertion, speak from this chair."

"Put on your hand a puppet that looks like the good girl part of you. And on your other hand, put on a puppet that looks like the bad girl part of you. Then have them talk to each other about how you feel about your dad."

"It seems that you have two parts of yourself that are tearing you apart. It is like your mother standing on one side of your shoulder saying 'Take it easy' and your father on the other shoulder saying, 'This is not good enough; work harder!' Here are two chairs. Sit in one and speak from the part of you that believes in your mother. Then move to the other chair and let the part of you that believes in your father's statement speak for yourself."

The Impact of Parts Dialogue From the Client's Point of View

- Clients bring the splits or parts of themselves into awareness.

- Clients learn to integrate the fragments of themselves.
- Clients deal with previously denied feelings.
- Clients experience insights that lead to change.

"EMPTY CHAIR": DEALING WITH UNFINISHED BUSINESS

Unfinished business is unresolved issues that cause people to relive incidents from the past. Often this reliving of the past is caused by unconscious urges to resolve the open wounds of the past. When helping clients deal with unfinished business, you can use *focused expressive therapy* (an extension of Gestalt therapy). One of the techniques of focused expressive therapy is the *empty chair exercise.* The empty chair exercise allows the client to bring someone who is unavailable (either geographically, physically, or emotionally) into the session so that the client can address some unfinished business with that person. By "directly confronting" that person within the safe confines of the therapist's office, the client is afforded an opportunity to move from feeling powerless and vulnerable to a sense of power and control, and then to separation and resolution.

Using Empty Chair Dialogue

Beginning counselors usually have difficulty deciding when to direct the client to change roles. Here is rule of thumb: When the client is sitting in his or her own chair, you want to escalate the emotions to its high point. As it ebbs down to a lower point, it is the time to change roles in the chairs. If a person is at a flat point in the exchange, it does no good to move back and forth in the chairs. Without escalating the emotion, the client falls into the trap of telling the story, which defeats the power of this technique. Direct the person to experience the feeling. Review the techniques of directives in the first section of this chapter.

Crying is clients' most common reaction to the Empty Chair experience. Crying is cathartic, and it usually makes clients feel better. Comment to them that it is okay to cry, that they are safe in the room, and to stay with those sad feelings for a while. New counselors often are concerned about reaching the right balance of tears without interrupting the process of the feeling. Realize that crying and emotions move in waves.

Some say that one session of empty chair is like eight sessions of regular counseling. For some clients this technique is comparable to stripping away the structure of the counseling process. The counselor is no longer engaged in conversation with the client. Rather, the counselor becomes a gentle coach in the background, offering encouragement to clients: to experience emotion, to reverse roles as they change chairs, and finally, to separate and to say "good-bye" to that person and that pain.

A note of consideration: If English is not the client's first language, or not the language the client would naturally speak to the person in the second chair, you and the client may want to consider using the native language. Otherwise, doing this exercise in a non-native language often makes clients slip into a cognitive and objective mode, preventing them from fully experiencing the emotion. Because this exercise is for the client, it may not be necessary for the counselor to know exactly what is being said. You should then use the non-verbal cues to direct role reversals.

Because of the newness of the technique for the client, it is important for the therapist to explain the rationale and structure and guide the client through this powerful experience. To guide the client, the therapist must know the how-to really well. Daldrup, Beutler, Engle, and Greenberg (1988) have outlined some principles as guidelines for conducting the empty chair. In the following, we explain each principle and give you some examples to illustrate each.

• Providing Rationale for Empty Chair Dialogue

Most clients have not experienced the empty chair dialogue. To help them become more receptive to this intervention, it is imperative to explain to the client why and how this exercise can be valuable.

Client:
"Now that my mother has died so suddenly, I am struggling with so many strong feelings that I can't tell her now."

Counselor:
"What are some of those strong feelings?"

Client:
"Well, I cannot quite put them into words clearly. I wish I could talk to her one more time."

Counselor:
"Julie, I know of one way for you to get a chance to talk with your mom without her being physically here. Would you like to try that?"

Client:
"Of course! If it is possible."

Counselor:
"Yes, it is possible. We could set up an exercise in this room right here right now. In this exercise, you can say everything that you have

wanted to say to her and have her listen fully to you. Here's how you can do that . . ."

Next example:

Client:
"I'm getting sick and tired! Each time she cuts me off when I try to talk to her. I really have tried to bring this up, but there is no talking to this woman."

Counselor:
"I can see how frustrated you are, Tom! You are trapped in 'unfinished business' because your ex doesn't want to cooperate. You feel like it will never work out."

Client:
"That's exactly how I feel. Really hopeless!"

Counselor:
"Okay. I'd like to suggest an empty chair exercise to bring her in today so that you can make her sit and listen to you without her cutting you off. Although you cannot change her attitude, you can address your feelings and let off steam. In this way, you can take care of your needs to express yourself and to be heard."

Another example:

Client:
"There are many things that happened 13 years ago when I was still a little girl. I cannot change them. But I wish I could."

Counselor:
"It seems like you feel that the past is pulling at you in the present. Maybe we need to go back to come to terms with those unresolved issues. We can use the empty chair exercise to go back to what has haunted you from 13 years ago. We can look at those things from the perspective of the child that you were then and the adult that you are now. In doing so, you can let go of the things that continue to drag you down."

c Making Process Suggestions: Do Not Ask Questions!

When shifting the client back and forth between the two chairs, it is important that you don't ask the client questions. Rather, just make statements about what you want her to do. You want to avoid asking questions so that the client can stay focused on her dialogue with the person in the other chair.

Questioning also can cause the clients to shift from emotional experiencing to an intellectual stance.

Examples:

> **"Tell your mother what you feel as you say that."**
>
> **"Tell your ex-wife what you heard in her voice."**
>
> **"Tell her what's behind your tears. Speak up for yourself."**
>
> **"Just tell your boss what actually humiliated you."**

c Giving Clients Permission and Support for Feeling Expression

Oftentimes clients feel guilty about expressing negative emotions. When negative emotions arise, clients tend to push them back. This prevents the empty chair exercise from reaching its climax. You can give permission for the free expression of your clients' feelings by saying:

> **"Stay with that anger!"**
>
> **"Allow yourself to go as far as you will with that sadness."**
>
> **"It's perfectly okay to cry. Cry as hard as you needs to!"**

c Using Role Reversal to Re-Evoke the Depth of Unfinished Feelings

Part of the essence of the empty chair exercise is role reversal. Role reversal evokes strong feelings from the past which have never been resolved. We want the buried feelings to be re-evoked because once evoked they have a better chance of being resolved.

> **"Julie, now sit over in this chair and be your mother. Say exactly what she would have said and done. (Allow the client sufficient time to finish this role). Now change back to your own chair and react to what she has said and done."**
>
> **"Change to the other chair, Tom, and be your ex-wife. Sit like she sits and talk in her voice. Say and do what she would say. (Pause) Now, change back and respond."**

c Directing the Client to Use "I" Language

Using the pronoun "you" or "it" is one way clients depersonalize intense or embarrassing feelings. Depersonalization is used often by people to avoid exposing their inner selves. Since the purpose of empty chair is to give authenticity back to people, it is therefore important to re-direct your clients to use "I" language to own up to their experiences.

"**Would you say 'I' instead of 'it'?**"

"**Try to use 'I' rather than a general 'you.'**"

c **Re-Directing Clients to Change Global Complaints to Specific Resentment**

Global complaints are difficult to resolve since they lack focus. When the clients present their issues in the empty chair with global language, you can re-direct them to describe the problems in specific behavioral terms.

"**Julie, instead of saying 'You never pay attention to me, Mom,' say 'I am hurt, Mom, when you get so caught up in your own world that you cannot be there for me.**"

"**Julie, rather than saying 'It make me mad to not have anyone around,' maybe you can say 'Mom, I feel abandoned when you are too depressed to be emotionally available to me.'**"

c **Helping Clients Develop Focusing Skills**

Focusing skills demonstrate one's abilities to first become aware of one's body sensations and then connect these sensations to one's emotions. Since the empty chair is all about resolving the unfinished business, developing this skill can bring previously unconscious emotions to the surface, enabling resolution of the past.

"**Be aware of your voice, Julie. Listen to how it trails off as you speak of the abandonment issue.**"

"**Tom, notice how you are shaking at this moment when you are talking about the affair.**"

"**Go back to the nausea and see how it feels as you express your anxiety.**"

c **Sharing Process Observation**

When the client shifts back and forth in the empty chair dialogue to work on unresolved issues, it is important to let him know what you have observed about his maladaptive behavior patterns or his mind-body disconnection. The empty chair exercise often brings out common behavior patterns that the client himself is not aware of. Sharing it with the client can help him break unwanted patterns that perpetuate his problems.

"Tom, I'm aware that you often hold your breath to fight back tears when you become angry."

"I hear the words of your anger, but I don't see the emotion."

"I'm aware that you fidget a lot whenever you mention your father."

c Feeding the Client Sentences as Try-Ons

When the client struggles with certain feelings and is unable to put them into words, or when the therapist notices some missing emotions, it is useful to guide the client with a suggestion or try-on.

"Tom, try out this sentence: 'I hate that you always put me down when all I did was just try to please you.'"

"See how this fits how you feel: 'I feel abandoned when you flirt with other women.'"

"Try out this line: 'I am afraid to tell you what I actually want from you.'"

"Try this out. If it does not feel right, you don't need to use it. 'Dad, I am deeply hurt by your cruelty.'"

c Making Hunches About Clients' Internal Struggles

When the client gets stuck in safe issues, unable to dive into the core of the problem, the therapist can interpret her behavior so that she can explore the problems at a deeper level.

"My sense is that the part of you that wants to get close to your father is in an intense power struggle with the part of you that wants to escape."

"My intuition tells me that you hide your emotions from your wife because of your fear of emotional intimacy. And this fear of intimacy has to do with your fear of being vulnerable."

c Disclosing Reactions to Client Behavior

Self-awareness involves realizing one's blind spots. One of people's blind spots is focusing on what others do to them without realizing how their behaviors might impact others. To increase the client's awareness about how his behavior impacts other people, the therapist can self-disclose her own internal reactions to the client's interpersonal patterns. Some of these internal reactions might be hard for the client to hear; therefore, it needs be used with sensitivity.

"I feel frustrated when you constantly place the burden of responsibility on other people."

"Tom, I feel powerless when you so often don't stand up for yourself and always put what other people want first."

"I feel miffed whenever you put yourself down and look to others to reassure you."

c Focusing on Incongruence

The therapist can also bring the client to higher awareness by pointing out the incongruence between her verbal and non-verbal behaviors.

"I'm aware of your angry words and polite smile. Try to say the words again without smiling them away."

"Tom, I hear you say you are not resentful and I see your teeth clinched and your eyelids twitching."

c Getting Clients in Touch With Constriction

Clients are often unaware that they hold emotions in their bodies. When they do, they tense their bodies up in various places, thus constricting their breathing and energy flow. The more they get out of touch with their emotions, the more likely they are to leave their issues unresolved. The therapist, therefore, should make notice of clients' constrictive behaviors and suggest they get in contact with whatever they are holding in.

"Julie, notice where in your body you are holding all your hurt and sadness. Stay with them for a moment. Don't try to run away from them."

"Slow down to listen to what you just said, Tom. It is perfectly okay to express whatever is grabbing you. Stay with what you just said for a while. Don't be afraid."

c Making Process Comments on a Client's Deflection of Emotions

When facing some difficult emotions, many clients unconsciously turn away from the empty chair dialogue and talk to the therapist. This deflection of emotions is a form of avoidance. When this happens, the therapist should comment on this avoidance behavior that she has observed in the client. Then she can suggest how the client can get back on track.

Client (turning from empty chair to the therapist):
"So you see how there is no way to talk to this woman."

Counselor:
"Why don't you tell her what you just told me?"

Client:
"Because it won't do any good. It's like putting your neck in the guillotine. If you want to say that to her, you can expect to get your head cut off."

Counselor:
"Tom, I'm very aware that you are avoiding her right now by making jokes with me." (This is the process comment.)

Client:
"But she cannot listen. She is so sure that she is right. And I am nobody to her. I just cannot put myself through the humiliation any more."

Counselor:
"Tom, here in this empty chair dialogue, you are the architect. You can create the kind of experience where you can have her fully listen to you so that you can take care of yourself."

Other examples of process comments:

"I'm aware that you just changed the subject."

"I notice that you are moving into your head and intellectualizing about why things are how they are today, rather than expressing your feelings."

c Helping a Client Finish the Cycle (the Ebb-and-Flow) of Crying

Crying typically happens in the empty chair dialogue when the old wounds are re-opened and the stuffed feelings are released. This cathartic process is very important in bringing the unfinished business to resolution. To facilitate the cathartic process, the therapist stays closely with the clients' emotional release and encourages her along the way to let it reach its climax.

The therapist should let this process continue until the client's body relaxes after reaching the emotional climax. A sense of quietness and peacefulness in the client is an indication that there are no more waves of emotion to be expressed at this time.

Client (sobbing):
"I miss you so much, Mom." (stronger rush of tears)

Counselor:
"It's okay to let out the tears that you have been building up."

Client:
"Mom, I love you very much. And I never got a chance to say good-bye. I feel like I will never get over the loss of you." (much crying as she talks)

Counselor:
"It's OK to let your tears go as far as they want to go."

Client:
(Bouts of tears and sobbing flow even more.)

Counselor:
"That's right, just let all that sadness come out. Let your tears flow out freely like the water in a river flowing into the ocean."

Client:
(Tears flow for a while. The sadness reaches its climax and then her body starts to relax.)

Counselor:
"That's it, Julie. Just notice how your body feels peaceful and relaxed after all the weight of your emotions have been lifted. Now just stay relaxed and be aware of the quietness you feel inside of yourself."

Client:
(Remains relaxed and serene while resting; then another wave of sadness overtakes her and another wave of tears floods her eyes.)

Counselor:
"That's okay. It is just another wave of sadness coming out from below. Just let it out like what you did before. Trust yourself and just let it happen. Let yourself ride and relax into those tears."

Client:
(Tears build to a climax and dissipate as before.)

The process of helping a client go through the ebb-and-flow of crying is demonstrated by the above example. When the cycle of crying is completed, some inner psychological healing will take place in due time.

c Closing the Experiment

After some sort of emotional climax has been reached and the old wounds have been cleansed, it is appropriate to close the dialogue through a symbolic ceremony of closure. A symbolic ceremony of closure can be anything that helps the client bring completion to the old business, for the time being. The clients can re-visit the issue anytime they choose, but they will start in a different place with greater strength.

Counselor:

"Julie, if you have a sense that you have finished your old business with Mom, I would suggest you do a sort of short ceremony to say goodbye to her. Would you like to do that?"

Client:

"All right. How will we do that?"

Counselor:

"Julie, you emotionally lost your Mom through her depression when you were a child. Then you physically lost her when she died suddenly. Today I want you to psychologically say goodbye to her in a symbolic ceremony by using the light from this candle to represent the loving part of your Mom that is shining inside of you."

Client (lights the candle):

"Well, Mom, I am ready to say goodbye to you for today. I realize that although you had a hard life and were unable to be there for me, you have still left me with that loving part of yourself that neither sickness nor death can take away from me. I am grateful for the time we spent together in the past and today. You will be always a part of me, and I will take care of myself as you would want me to. (Client appears surprised and relieved by the outcome of this empty chair dialogue)."

Counselor:

"If you need to, allow yourself to stay with this gratitude and love for as long as can."

Another example:

Counselor:

"Okay, Tom. Are you ready to stop there for today?"

Client:

"Yes, I am. I feel really good about finally confronting her."

Counselor:

"Now say goodbye to your ex-wife for now. We may want to come back to her later."

Client:

"I cannot believe that I was able to talk to her about my humiliation and resentment toward her betrayal. It's a sense of relief!"

Counselor:

"Anything you want to say to her before you say goodbye, Tom?"

The Impact of Empty Chair Technique From the Client's Point of View

- Clients reenact past scenes and gain corrective emotional experiences.
- Clients experience how they impact other people.
- Clients learn to stand up for themselves in situations where they were previously unable to do so.
- Clients resolve unfinished business in their lives.
- Clients experience their own power.

REFLEXIVE QUESTIONS

Your beliefs and concepts about human beings, counseling, and psychotherapy shape the questions your ask of your clients. If you believe that counseling is to correct pathology and resolve an ingrained dark past, you tend to ask for the details of the pathology and the dark past. If you believe counseling is to help generate clients' new sense of self and a more fulfilling way of life, then you tend to ask for details that explain what the client would like his or her self-story to be. This latter view characterizes *narrative therapy.*

As you have mentioned previously, two types of questions are used in counseling. *Probing* (as described in Chapter 4), as a basic skill, is used to help the counselor *gather information,* whereas the *reflexive question* (Tomm, 1987, 1988), an advanced skill, is used to facilitate the client to *generate experience of preferred realities* (Freedman & Combs, 1996). This section covers reflexive questions. What are Reflexive Questions?

First, you need to know what reflexivity is about. Reflexivity enables clients to observe themselves and to examine the factors (perceptions, actions, options, and meanings) that shape their own experiences. Therefore, reflexive questions are questions that help clients to achieve self-examination, self-awakening, and self-discovery.

Reflexive questions are formulated to trigger clients to reflect on the implications of their current perceptions and actions and to consider new options and meanings (Tomm, 1988). Reflexive questions facilitate self-healing by generating new meanings for clients, and by helping them produce constructive patterns of cognition and behavior on their own. In the counseling process, you can use reflexive questions to enable clients to see new possibilities. It is respectful of the client's autonomy and resources. In narrative therapy, reflexive questions are important vehicles for client growth.

Using Reflexive Questions

This section focuses on five types of reflexive questions that generate and heal. The ideas are inspired by Tomm (1987).

✔ Future-Oriented Reflexive Questions
✔ Unexpected Reflexive Questions
✔ Embedded-Suggestion Questions
✔ Normalization Questions
✔ Questions Introducing Hypotheses

Future-Oriented Reflexive Questions

Future-oriented reflexive questions ask clients to imagine what would happen if they were to change in the future. The use of *when* rather than *if* is consequential. When you use *when,* it suggests to clients that change will happen; it is only a matter of when. But if you use *if,* then it suggests some doubt regarding whether or not the change will actually take place. Future-oriented reflexive questions plant seeds of preferred situations in clients' minds so that the images of these preferred situations are visualized in their minds' eyes. When clients can visualize the change, the change is more likely to occur.

Examples:

"When (not if) you **face your problem with alcohol, what will be the first thing to happen?"**

"When you move out of your mom's house, how will your life be different?"

"How much more relaxed will you feel by June?"

"Who will be happiest when you give up your addiction?"

"Who will be your greatest supporter when you earn your bachelor's degree?"

"When *(not if) you* **start to lose weight, who will be the first to notice?"**

"How will your family show their gratitude in response to your change?"

"How will your relationship with your husband be different when you become more open?"

"Who would be the first to celebrate your success in change?"

"If you could change one thing in your job, what would that one thing be?"

"How would you like things to turn out for you in five years?"

"I can see that you are feeling really angry right now. How would you like things with your boss to change?"

Unexpected Reflexive Questions

Unexpected reflexive questions catch clients off guard. In these questions, behaviors and inner processes are personified in a way that is unexpected so that change is more likely. In addition, it is a paradox that when a taboo subject is talked about, the taboo loses its grasping power. After taboo subjects are brought out to the sunlight, they disintegrate.

> **"How is it that you have not destroyed yourself before this?"**

> **"What patterns of your behavior need to die?"**

> **"What ideas and thoughts do you need to kill off in order for you to feel better?"**

> **"What feelings need to be buried for you to move on?"**

> **"What feelings about your body image need to be purged?"**

> **"What learning about violence as a solution needs to be beaten out of you?"**

> **"What was it that you were trying to cut away in your self-mutilation?"**

Embedded-Suggestion Questions

Embedded-suggestion reflexive questions have a suggestion built within the questions. These questions are almost hypnotic in nature in that they offer subliminal solutions or suggestions that become implanted in clients' unconsciousness. These suggestions should be positive and solution-oriented in nature. By building a solution within a question, the therapist can offer a more indirect intervention to client problems. See following examples:

> **"If you were to tell her how insulted you feel about her infidelity, what do you imagine she would do?"**

> **"Imagine that your boss wants to direct the project but he isn't sure if you are ready, how would you show him that you were strong enough to do the work?"**

> **"When you decided to start overeating, what was the hole that you were trying to fill?"**

> **"If the long-standing argument between you and your mom is to be ameliorated, who would be most ready to apologize?"**

Other examples:

> **"How would it be if you took your comic persona off and let yourself be vulnerable? How would you react in that incident you described?"**

"What would happen if you were to sit down with your daughter and not point your finger at her for doing drugs; but just say that 'I have a question I have had within me for years that is eating away at me. I am angry and extremely frightened for you. And I don't know where it is coming from. I have a sense that you have a really deep anger toward me.' What would happen if you were to verbalize these ideas to her?"

Normalization Questions

Normalization reflexive questions are asked in a way that lets clients know that they are not alone in their experiences. This type of question often helps clients feel relieved that they are not alone in their suffering because inherent in the questions is the fact that clients' problems are normal. Consider the following examples:

"Everybody has problems dealing with loss. When did you first realize that you were not alone in your desperation?"

"Many people have had suicidal thoughts at some time during their lives. Were you surprised to hear this?"

"If you realized how common these issues are, would you be more willing to take a courageous look at how they have affected your life?"

"Would you be surprised to learn that many abused women have the same feelings of worthlessness that you have expressed?"

Questions Introducing Hypotheses

Questions that introduce hypotheses reframe the old and ineffective theories developed by clients about why they react in certain ways. This reframing offers a more positive interpretation or hypothesis about patterns of behavior that fits better with a client's reality and leads to solutions. Often clients attribute their problems to negative self traits and personality defects. This type of attribution is self-defeating. To reverse this self-defeating attribution, you can use a question that introduces a new hypothesis suggesting a new paradigm for viewing the cause of the problem. When the view of the cause of the problem is changed, solutions come easier.

Examples:

"If you do get depressed to cover up your vulnerability and you just can't reach in to connect with your underlying anger, do you see yourself as weak and helpless, or do you see yourself as simply overly considerate of other people's feelings, or perhaps, even as oppressed by your own desire to please?"

(Continued) **"In order for the assertive part of you to grow naturally, what kind of self-assurance and nurturing does that part of you need the most?"**

The Impact of Reflexive Questions From the Client's Point of View:

- Clients are able to see new possibilities.
- Clients are led to envision a more effective life.
- Clients are liberated to talk about taboo subjects.
- Clients experience subliminal suggestive messages regarding their recovery.
- Clients feel that their problems are normal and their sense of shame is reduced.

NARRATIVE STEPS FOR CO-CONSTRUCTING CHANGE WITH CLIENTS: USING REFLEXIVE QUESTIONS

You have learned how to use reflexive questions to generate a new self-identity and a sense of competency in the last section. Now it's time to ask the question, "When and how do I apply them in the process of counseling?" This chapter answers this question.

The process of co-constructing change with a client goes beyond basic counseling skills. It may require the use of a series of reflexive questions as is typical in narrative therapy. It may take several sessions to complete the whole process of co-constructing change with a client. To make it easy to learn, this chapter will break this process down into several steps. However, these steps are not meant to represent a linear process. You may need to loop back to some earlier steps at times.

Note: To avoid being too cognitive, you need to follow up each reflexive question with empathic responses, such as paraphrasing, reflection of feelings, perception checking, summarization, advanced empathy, immediacy, and self-disclosure.

Using Narrative Steps

Narrative steps for co-constructing client change include:

✔Empathizing with the Client's Story
✔Noticing Themes or Behavior Coping Patterns
✔Sharing the Themes with the Client

✔Mapping Out the Impact of the Client's Self-Defeating Coping Patterns
✔Tracing Past or Current Influences
✔Searching for Unique Outcomes
✔Planting the Seeds for Preferred Outcomes
✔Client Performing the Preferred Narrative

The following sections describe these steps:

1. Empathizing With the Client's Story

Use all empathic responses (as specified in Chapter 3) to achieve active listening. The counselor should spend adequate time getting to know the client's problem in context and getting to know client's life background. The time needed to get to know a client cannot be underestimated. This is an ongoing process.

2. Noticing Themes or Behavior Coping Patterns

While listening to a client's story and conveying empathy to the client, you need to keep the common thread of the client's stories in your mind. This internal processing is very important if the counseling process is to go to a deeper level. See the Theme Analysis section in Chapter Nine "Case Conceptualization," for more on how to notice common threads and themes.

The purpose of a theme analysis is not to identify a client's ineffective behaviors and use them to place blame. Rather, the purpose is *to name* the ineffective behaviors that are oppressive to the client and, later, *to map their influences* on the client's life.

3. Advanced Empathizing: Sharing the Themes With the Client

After the counselor recognizes some threads—positive or negative—that are significant in the client's story, it is important to convey this insight to the client when the timing is right. You can use advanced empathy (see Chapter 6) to do that. When you identify the theme with the client, it brings seemingly fragmented pieces of a story into a meaningful perspective.

When sharing a self-defeating theme with a client, describe the pattern as if it is "a powerful enemy with malevolent intent and a crafty, seductive, deceitful character, or else a well-intended but misguided, controlling life manager" (Griffith and Griffith, 1994, p. 115). This kind of language helps the client separate clearly the problems from his or her sense of self or self-identity.

Examples:

"From the several events you shared, it seems that you find it easy at times to slip into the trap of letting other people make decisions for you."

"This thread seems to come up again and again, that is, silencing yourself in groups seems to tyrannize you in many ways."

4. Mapping Out the Impact of the Client's Self-Defeating Coping Pattern

In this step, you work to map out a detailed picture about the impact of clients' ineffective coping patterns on their emotional and social lives. This shows clients how their themes are impacting many parts of their lives without their being aware of it.

Examples:

"How does this pattern of letting others make decisions for you influence your feeling about yourself?"

"How does this pattern of silencing yourself in groups impact your relationship with others?"

"When depression recruited you into the life style of isolation, how did it affect your relationship with your husband?"

"What effects have the seduction of drug use had on your family?"

"How does befriending the fear of commitment affect your relationship with yourself?"

5. Tracing Past or Current Influences That Recruit the Client Into the Pattern

After identifying themes and mapping their impact on clients, it is important to follow up with questions that help clients gain insight into how they get caught up in these patterns in the first place. When they understand how the problems started, they are often able to see that their ineffective coping behaviors are no longer useful. This exploration on the external influences liberates the clients from seeing themselves as pathological.

Examples:

"How does the pattern of letting other people make decisions for you sneak into your life?"

"What influencing factors pushed you into the pattern of lack of assertiveness in the group?"

"How does fear try to get a hold of you?"

"What past experiences or training recruited you into this pattern of seeing yourself so low?"

"How do you think that the notion in our society that women should be subservient to their husbands has contributed to the problem you have with your husband? How has this contributed to your depression?"

6. Searching for Unique Outcomes (White, 1989)

Up to this step, the focus has been on the problems. You have to analyze the problem just as a soldier would analyze an enemy. Therefore, in the initial stages, problem talk predominates most of the counseling process. Starting from this step, the emphasis will take a turn. To help clients re-author their lives, problem talk is not the key, but rather their sense of self-efficacy is. You need to help clients re-write the tales they tell about themselves, in other words, their self-concept, self-images, self-narratives, and their outdated and outlived scripts. The key is to help clients change their personal myths. When self-narratives are altered, behavioral change follows. How do you co-author new narratives with clients? In essence, you need to scour for *exceptions* to the problematic patterns or to search for *the counter-story* of the problem (see Unique Outcome Analysis in Chapter 9 Case Conceptualization). In every story clients tell, there are other stories that get repressed or negated. These repressed stories usually are not prominent in the information clients tell us. They represent the exceptions or the counter-story to the problems that dominate clients' views of themselves. You can use questions to draw out unnoticed narratives about clients. That is, you pull from the background to the forefront these exceptions or counter-stories. The goal of asking these questions is to make these exceptions or counter-stories become the leading story or motif in the clients' lives. When the leading story changes from problem-dominated themes to strength-dominated themes, then the clients' self-efficacy will improve.

Examples:

> **"Is there any situation or any time in your life when you managed to defy the seduction of alcohol?"**
>
> **"In what other ways have you stood up against this compulsion to overeat and not let it push you around?"**
>
> **"Has there ever been a time when your addiction tried to overcome you, but you were able to resist its influence?"**
>
> **"Can you tell me about other times or moments when you rose above the pull of the waves of depression?"**

7. Planting the Seeds for Preferred Outcomes (White, 1989)

In this step, you and the client together invent the *preferred way of living* or the *preferred self-identity* of the client. The preferred self-identity is the higher self or possible self to which the client aspires. One task of any therapy is to help the client reach this higher self. How do you do this? The key is for the therapist to use the reflexive questions (Tomm, 1987, 1988) you learned (see the section of Reflexive Questions in this chapter) to draw out as rich, detailed and meaningful as possible a description of the preferred self-narrative (Freed-man and Combs, 1996). These questions help to consolidate the new narratives re-authored by client and counselor. In so doing, the seeds for growth of the preferred self or higher self are planted in the client's unconsciousness.

"What does it tell about you that you are able to resist the seduction of the self mutilation and start to reclaim your own body's integrity?"

"What will your life be like when you continue to stand up against the oppression of your boss's emotional abuse and claim your own voice?"

"What do you think you might discover about yourself when you manage not to be pushed around by alcohol when others would give in to its tyranny?"

"If you were to imagine this desired direction of becoming peaceful, what would be the first sign that you are venturing into a life of balance?

"Who will be the first person to notice that you have had victory over the tyranny of performance anxiety?"

"Who is likely to be the audience for your new voice and lifestyle of self love?"

"What are you likely to feel when you discover that you have over-thrown the fear of facing your illness?"

"How might your life look different if you were to choose to reach out rather than staying isolated?

8. Client Performing the Preferred Narrative

In Step 6 you conscientiously used reflexive questions to draw out new narratives from clients who identify buried resources and strengths; in Step 7, you implanted in clients' minds new ways of living and experiencing them-selves. By this time, clients should be immersed in the new narrative about themselves. These new narratives will inevitably be performed in their outside lives. As Freedman and Combs (1996, p. 87) said, "Once you say it out loud, it's more real. Then you do it."

The Impact of Narrative Steps From the Client's Point of View

- Clients come to see themes in their ineffective behaviors.
- Fragmented pieces of the client's story are given meaning.
- Clients learn to separate their problems from their self-identities.
- Clients recognize how ineffective coping patterns have impacted their lives.

- Clients understand that their problems are embedded in the larger context of past and present social and political environments.
- Clients learn to look more objectively at their problems and to find solutions.
- Clients invent a preferred way of living, a preferred identity, to which they aspire.

THE BODY AWARENESS TECHNIQUE

For clients who are overly cognitive or those who are body-alienated, we can use the body awareness technique to help them gain access to their feelings, which may otherwise prove to be difficult. Body awareness can bypass the need for language, which sometimes gets in the way of getting in touch with the real issues of the client. The information obtained through this exercise can give direction for further therapy work.

Using Body Awareness

The basic form of invitation to body awareness can be represented by an example provided by Smith (1985):

> Close your eyes and just relax for a few moments. Breathe comfortably. (Pause.) (Repeat the directions to relax and then pause until the client seems to be involved in the exercise.) Check out your body to see what you find. Note anything in your body which calls attention to itself. Just monitor your body, inch by inch, from tips of your toes to the top of your head and down to the tips of your fingers. In particular, note any hot spots, cold spots, tight or tense muscles, pains, tingling, or anything happening in your body. Don't try to edit or change anything, just be aware and note what is happening. (Pause for a minute or two.) Take your time. When you are finished, open your eyes (Wait until the client opens her or his eyes.). (p. 107)

After this exercise, ask the client to describe what he or she has discovered. The discovery of body phenomena can then be used as material for further therapy work.

Many other therapies also deal with body techniques. These techniques are based on the idea that many emotions, memories, and past experiences are stored in the body; therefore, movement and exploration of the body are the most direct ways of reaching material that has been repressed. Also, repeated experiences can form circuits in the nervous system that automatically cause the body to react in certain, unhealthy ways when similar situations arise.

Body techniques have been used in Eastern religions for thousands of years, but have been popularized in the U.S. recently with the work of Herbert Benson (1975) in his book, *The Relaxation Response.* This book laid the foundation for the various forms of systematic relaxation that have been used to treat phobias and anxiety, including panic attacks. Additionally, rolfing, body massage, yoga, and tai chi are now used in combination with traditional therapy to help people get in touch with emotions and memories stored deep within their bodies.

Some repressed emotions are so deeply buried that traditional talk therapies will not begin to release them. After repressed emotions and memories have been brought into consciousness, then they can be dealt with on cognitive and behavioral levels. It is only through body awareness that progress can be made.

Recent attention has centered on whether or not regained memories are false. Generally, if memories involve bodily reactions such as vomiting, muscle contractions, and flashbacks, the memories are real. Therapists should not suggest the possibility that clients have repressed their memories. Further, hypnosis and drugs should never be given to clients to help them recall memories.

The body is an important part in the mind-body connection, and attention must be paid to symptoms presented in the body. Also, clients can improve the speed of recovery by giving attention to their physical being. Of course, it is necessary to be aware of the ethical issues involved in physical contact with clients. Body techniques can be very helpful, when used with respect for client-counselor boundary issues.

The Impact of Body Awareness From the Client's Point of View

- Clients gain access to feelings that they didn't originally have.
- Clients' emotions, memories, past experiences that are stored in the body may be released.
- Clients learn to relax in situations that previously would have caused them anxiety.
- Clients' recovery rate improve when they are treated holistically.

THE "YES" SET

Have you ever worked with a client who is apathetic? Such clients will give you one word answers and slouch down in the chair with their arms folded across their chests. Their postures and verbal expression say, "I dare you to fix me." As a result, you feel deeply dejected. When working with this kind of

skeptical and unmotivated client, counselors needs to employ certain intervention techniques early in the course of counseling. A powerful technique to
help clients overcome resistance, used frequently by the Ericksonian
approach, is called the "Yes" set (Dolan, 1985). A "Yes" set is a state of mind
that features agreement and deep acceptance. When clients are in this "Yes"
mind set, they will be receptive to your therapeutic work.

Using the "Yes" Set

The way to exercise the Ericksonian's "Yes"set intervention technique is to
first acknowledge and reflect the clients' experience or shared current experiences. This first step is also called *"truism"* (Dolan, 1985, p. 45). In truism,
you simply reflect or employ current truths about the client or about shared
experiences. To be able to employ truisms, you need to develop an attitude of
deep appreciation and compassion for the client. Repeated use of truisms with
resistant clients may make them bored. Then this boredom makes it easy for
them to get on to the second step, which is the hard work of therapy. So the
first step of truism paves the way for the client to be in a "Yes" mentality for
the second step. The client is ready to work.

The following example is an excerpt from Dolan (1985, p. 47). We have
chosen to use this example in totality because it vividly illustrates the "Yes"
set technique.

> Therapist:
> **"Your name is Harry."**
>
> Client:
> (Client nods yes.)
>
> Therapist:
> **"We've spoken on the phone, but this is the first time you've come to my
> office."**
>
> Client:
> (Client nods yes.)
>
> Therapist:
> **"You told me on the phone that you've felt frustrated by your previous
> experiences in therapy."**
>
> Client:
> (nodding yes) "That's right."
>
> Therapist:
> **"And now it is two o'clock on Tuesday afternoon and you're here and
> I'm here..."**
>
> Client:
> (Client nods, visibly relaxes, and adjusts body in chair into more comfortable
> position.)

Therapist:
"And you're sitting in that tan chair and I'm in this brown chair, the clock is ticking, and outside some birds are singing *(comment on shared ongoing experience).***"**

Client:
(Client begins to look somewhat impatient, begins to play with a paper clip he picks up from the adjoining table. He looks at the therapist with an expression of *expectancy and curiosity.*)

Therapist:
"And I am wondering if you'd be willing to tell me just exactly how you would like things to be for you in your life after completing this therapy together..."

Client:
"The changes I'd like to see happen are..."*

The above example illustrate how the use of truism differs from basic empathy or immediacy. In basic empathy, you reflect client's feelings or implied meanings without the sense of absurdity. In immediacy, you reflect the client's non-verbal behaviors or the relationship between you and the client. However, when using truisms, you make statements about the client and the situation that are so plainly obvious that it becomes humorous and absurd. After several truism statements like this, the client becomes bored, or even angry, with the obvious. Since apathy and anger are mutually exclusive, the anger mentally shifts the client to a desire to move forward to real work.

The Impact of the "Yes" Set From the Client's Point of View

- Unmotivated clients become motivated to work without being confronted about their resistance.
- Clients become receptive to the therapeutic direction.

THE "NO" SET: DEALING WITH THE MISMATCHER

Every now and then, you will encounter a client who responds to your suggestions with a constant "No." This *repetitive pattern of disagreement* in the client makes the progress of counseling impossible. You should not consider this kind of negativity as a pathology, but rather as the way the client's mind

---

*Copyright 1985 from *A Path With a Heart: Ericksonian Utilization With Resistant and Chronic Clients* by Dolan. Reproduced by permission of Taylor & Francis, Inc., http://www.routledge-ny.com.

works. Indeed, 35 percent of people in the population operate from this kind of disagreement mind set; and the name for these people is *"mismatchers"* (Robbins, 1986, p. 261). The mismatcher's mind sees difficulties, sees how things don't work, and sees all sorts of problems.

Mismatchers are valuable in offering overlooked flaws in implementing projects. But when they employ that very mind set in interpersonal relationships, people hate them. And when they show up in the counseling room, you feel disheartened and miserable for their all-encompassing negativity. You suffer. How do you work with mismatcher clients?

Again we come back to an intervention technique employed by the Ericksonian approach. It is called *the "No" set* (Dolan, 1985). This is how it works: Repeat or reflect the client's pattern of negation. Then follow it with your own negation question at the end of the response.

Using the "No" Set

The utilization of client negation is likely to create a bridge of acceptance between the client and the counselor, leading the client to change a "No" mind set into a "Yes" mind set. When the client changes to the "Yes" mind set, then you can use truisms (reflective skills), followed by a negation question. This method works well with clients who are very experienced and masterful in resistance (Dolan, 1985).

Following are several sets of examples excerpted from Dolan (1985)*. We heavily quote Dolan's work because they are the best illustrations that we could ever find.

Client:
"It was very inconvenient for me to come here today, and I'm not feeling very hopeful about coming to therapy."

Therapist:
"You have had some past experiences that cause you to feel not very hopeful about therapy (repeat client's negation), and yet despite the inconvenience (repeat client's negation), you had the courtesy to drive here and keep this appointment anyway, didn't you (end in negation question)?"

Client:
"Yes, I did." (Dolan, 1985, p. 51–52)

---

*Copyright 1985 from *A Path With a Heart: Ericksonian Utilization With Resistant and Chronic Clients* by Dolan. Reproduced by permission of Taylor & Francis, Inc., http://www.routledge-ny.com.

The counselor in the above example has successfully changed the client from a "No" mind set to a "Yes" mind set.

The following example demonstrates how probing skills fail to work with a chronic mismatcher:

Client:
"It doesn't seem like anyone can help me . . . it all seems hopeless."

Therapist:
"What is it that you would most like help with?"

Client:
"I really don't know. It feels like everything is going wrong in my life right now."

Therapist:
"Can you give me some examples?"

Client:
"Well, I don't know where to start." (Dolan, 1985, p. 55)

The therapist in the preceding example tried to use probing to help the client open up but failed. The therapist soon realized that the client had a repetitive pattern of negation. An early intervention technique — the "No" set — is thus employed for the rest of the session. The following examples are from the later parts of the session. Although it takes a long series of the "No" set to establish the therapeutic trust, it really pays off.

Therapist:
"There's a lot that you feel is going wrong right now (truism) and you don't (negation) know where to begin to describe it."

Client:
(sighs) "Yeah…"

Therapist:
"And you seem to be feeling pretty weary (truism) and I'm wondering where we can start that won't be as difficult as previously (negation)."

Client:
"I don't mind it being difficult if it works in the long run. I'm just tired of the way things are going and have been going."

Therapist:
"You are tired of the way things are (truism, conveys acceptance) and maybe you're even somewhat worried that things could actually get worse. (exaggeration of client's negative frame) Are you not (negation question)?"

Client:
(nods) "That's right."

Therapist:
"And now we are sitting here together (truism), and it's less than five minutes into this session (truism), isn't it (negation question)?"

Client:
(looking puzzled) "That's right — yes."

Therapist:
"And you are in your thirties still (truism), isn't that right (negation question)?"

Client:
"Yes."

Therapist:
"And you have been suffering through this divorce and other problems for a long time now (truism), haven't you (negation question)?"

Client:
"Yes It's been over three years, and it really hurts (tears come into her eyes)."

Therapist:
"And you would like to be able to realistically look forward to some happy times in the future (truism), would you not (negation question)?"

Client:
(breathes deeply and momentarily relaxes body posture) "I sure would."

Therapist:
"You've been hurting for a long time now (client nods) you're tired of the pain(client nods) you're still only in your thirties (client nods) and you would like to be able to enjoy your life more(client nods) which is the purpose of being here today(client nods) . . . so why not begin by letting yourself start to think about how you would be feeling and spending your time at the end of successful therapy?"

Client:
(closes eyes for a few seconds before beginning to speak) "Well, I wouldn't be thinking about Jeff all the time ... I'd have a job that I liked, a more comfortable place to live, and I wouldn't be overweight like I am right now. And I ... hopefully, would have some new friends. Maybe I'd be dating someone."

Therapist:
"When you think of that, how does that make you feel?"

Client:
"Pretty good... except for the losing weight part. That seems pretty near hopeless. The more I feel bad, the more I eat, and then I feel bad because I'm fat and there it goes again (shrugs, throws hands in the air and lets them fall on her lap in an energetic and exaggerated fashion)." (Note: client's energetic body movement indicates that the 'yes' set is fully established.)

Therapist:
"So it would be a pretty amazing experience for you to actually lose the extra weight as well as resolve the other problems too, wouldn't it?"

Client:
(smiles) "It sure would."

Therapist:
"Well, why not start by telling me a little about how you've been spending your time and how you've been feeling this week."

Client:
"Okay. Well, Monday I saw my attorney. The divorce date is finally a week from next Tuesday. Ever since then I've been pretty much just sitting around my apartment doing nothing. I suppose I should feel happy that it's almost over. I truly want the divorce. But I feel this horrible sadness, like 'What kind of life is this I'm living?' I'm not dating anyone. I hate my job, I've spent the last three years fighting with my ex-husband over legal details. I don't seem to know where I'm going anymore . . . I want to find out. I want to take charge of my life." (Dolan, 1985, p. 55–56)

The above example is a powerful illustration of how a resistant client can be changed to a cooperative client. The therapist has successfully changed the client's "No" mind set to a "Yes" mind set by mirroring the client's pattern of negation and by using truisms. The client has opened up, and has used more positive language. The rest of the therapy will be less difficult within this mind frame.

The Impact of the "No" Set From the Client's Point of View

- Clients feel totally accepted because the therapist creates a bridge of acceptance by repeating the client's negation pattern.
- Clients relax their defenses and become more open to change.
- Clients are motivated to change without being directly confronted about their resistance.
- Clients make an unconscious shift toward a more positive attitude.

CHAPTER EIGHT

TERMINATION SKILLS

T he last stage of the counseling process is the Termination Stage. Your tasks in this stage include helping clients deal with a sense of loss and separation anxiety, evaluate progress, anticipate future happenings, and bring closure to therapy.

Saying good-bye is difficult for many people. For this reason, many people turn saying good-bye" into a farewell party where grief can be expressed in an atmosphere filled with jokes, noises, and foods. When the emotions associated with separation and loss are not dealt with, the emotional stress can be converted into physical illness, stress in relationships, problems at work, and addictions. Separating from the therapist can bring back the anxiety clients associate with prior losses. Because some clients have trouble in saying "good-bye," they simply don't show up at the last meeting. It is important that clients learn how to say good-bye to their counselors so that they can transfer this skill to other life settings. Counselors can guide the termination into an empowering and liberating process.

APPLYING TERMINATION SKILLS

The following are specific termination skills that are helpful in allowing clients to separate from the therapist and move on with their lives. These skills include:

- Dealing with feelings of separation
- Assessing the progress
- Reviewing the counseling experience
- Giving and receiving feedback
- Carrying learning further
- Saying goodbye

Dealing With Feelings of Separation Before Termination

Invite clients to express their reactions (fears or concerns, sense of loss, grief) about separation from the therapeutic relationship.

> "I see you are ready to move on with your life, so that means our counseling will be terminating very soon. How do you feel about ending counseling?"

> "I sense that you are having some strong feelings about ending our counseling relationship. Would you like to talk about it?"

Assessing the Progress

Asking assessing questions at the end of the therapeutic relationship reminds clients that they have come a long way since they first began. This brings to clients hope, a sense of celebration, and a feeling of self-confidence that they will be able to move forward on their own. One of the techniques that is helpful in assessing progress in the *scaling question:*

> "On a scale of 10, if 0 indicates an extreme sense of hopelessness, powerlessness and the worst sense of yourself, and 10 indicates an optimal sense of confidence, feeling good about yourself and trust in life, where were you when you first came in? And where are you now?"

Reviewing the Counseling Experience

In addition to using scaling questions to assess progress, it is important to review clients' counseling experiences to consolidate their learning and progress. Therapists can ask specific questions to bring out the details of a client's learning.

> "How has counseling been important for you?"

> "When you say that you have grown a lot, what are some of the changes you have seen in yourself?"

> "What were the highlights of the counseling experience for you?"

> "What were some specific things that you became aware of about your lifestyle, attitudes, and relationships with others?"

Giving and Receiving Feedback

Giving clients feedback helps them gain an objective view of what they have accomplished in therapy and how you experience them as persons. In everyday conversation, people rarely give each other honest feedback. They may give each other compliments or make superficial observations, but seldom do they give and receive meaningful, constructive observations about how they are seen by others. Real feedback gives clients information that they do not ordinarily receive. Feedback is a gift from the therapist.

"This is what I have seen in you..."

"These are things I hope you will think about doing for yourself..."

You can also request feedback from your clients about how you are viewed. This is not only helpful for you, but it also helps clients feel respected because their opinions are so valued. Clients also benefit from giving feedback because in doing so, they must summarize what they have experienced and they must trust their feelings. Giving feedback helps bring closure to the counseling experience.

"I would like to hear from you some feedback about my working style. What has been most helpful for you? What has been least helpful for you? What would you like me to do differently?"

Carrying Learning Further

When you and your clients terminate the counseling relationship, it is always a goal that the learning the client has gained in counseling will continue throughout life. When asked questions that require looking into the future, clients can imagine how their lives will be enhanced as they continue their personal growth process.

"What will your life be like when you continue the growth you experienced in counseling?"

"How will you help yourself to continue the growth you experienced here after termination?"

"If you were to be a consultant for someone who experienced a difficulty similar to yours, what wisdom would you share with him or her?"

"I would like to co-create a certificate for you as an indication that you have overcome the effect of depression. What would you write on the certificate about yourself?"

Saying Goodbye by Mutually Sharing Appreciation and Regret

The last piece of bringing closure to the counseling relationship is to mutually express appreciation of the other person and regret at not being able to continue the relationship. Although this part may be awkward, when done from the heart, it brings humanity and dignity to both parties. Not only do clients have difficulty separating from their counselors, sometimes counselors also have difficulty terminating with their clients. They may even wish to phone just to find out how the clients are doing. However, this is not a wise practice because it shows dependency on the part of the counselor. Calling clients has the effect of encouraging them to come back for unnecessary sessions that are needed, indeed, more by the therapist than by the clients.

One way to achieve an emotional closure with clients is to share your appreciation and regret with your clients.

You can share appreciation and regret by saying:

"I want you to know that I deeply appreciate your sharing yourself with me. I have enjoyed seeing you over the past few months and I will miss our interaction."

"Thank you for trusting me and allowing me to get to know you as a person. I have come to deeply admire your courage and integrity in your struggle and the growth you have made. I will miss talking with you."

The client may share appreciation and regret. If the client is unable to express his or her feelings at the time of termination, you as the counselor, understanding that the unspoken words often convey more meaning than verbalization, should allow a period of silence. If the client cries, again you should wait patiently until the tears subside. Tears do not indicate that additional sessions are needed, but just that the client is touched by the emotions of termination.

Impact of Successful Termination From the Client's Point of View

- Clients deal with their sense of loss and separation anxiety at the end of therapy.
- Clients can celebrate the progress they have made in therapy.
- Clients gain insight by reviewing the whole counseling process.
- Clients receive honest final feedback from the therapist.
- Clients look into the future to imagine further personal growth.
- Clients can process unfinished business.
- Clients learn to end a relationship in a positive and hopeful way.

CHAPTER NINE

CASE CONCEPTUALIZATION: THE COVERT SKILLS

Working with clients involves attending to relevant information, forming and testing a working hypothesis, and formulating an appropriate intervention strategy. In this process, you formulate an overall picture of how clients' problems are formed and maintained, as well as how change can be initiated. This is a covert process. This covert process is usually called *case conceptualization.* It determines the direction and effectiveness of counseling. It is covert because it is done in the head of the counselor, often during the session for experienced counselors and after the session for beginning counselors.

In comparison, the reflective listening skills, influencing skills, and the intervention techniques we have already learned are the *overt* competencies that a counselor performs in the session. They are overt because they are seen and heard in the opening of the session. Mastering only the overt skills does not guarantee effectiveness in counseling. Skill development needs to go hand-in-hand with case conceptualization. The way you conceptualize the case usually directs the ways you navigate the counseling process.

Because case conceptualization is done in the counselor's head, it is impossible for beginning counselors to observe and understand it. However, certain structured exercises can help beginning counselors see some light in the darkness. This chapter is devoted to some simple exercises for case conceptualization:

- Theme analysis
- Contextual analysis
- Unique outcome analysis
- Preferred outcome analysis
- How to write case notes

THEME ANALYSIS:
BASIC CASE CONCEPTUALIZATION

During the initial stage of counseling, it is helpful to do a theme analysis to help yourself map out your client's struggles. Theme analysis helps you gain focus and increase effectiveness in the helping process.

A theme in counseling sessions usually consists of three components:

✔The common thread
✔The coping pattern
✔The vicious cycle

• The Common Thread

The first step of basic case conceptualization is to highlight the thread that runs through different sessions, or the thread that connects islands. *The common thread is usually the underlying feelings or issues resulting from overwhelming life circumstances.* These underlying feelings are usually more profound than the presenting problem. The presenting problems are usually the symptoms or surfaces of the real issues, whereas the underlying feelings are often associated with frustrated fundamental needs. Therefore, you need to pay more attention to the threads of feelings that run through different sessions than merely to the initial problems that the client states.

• The Coping Patterns

The second step of basic case conceptualization is to observe the behaviors used by the client to cope with the underlying issues or feelings. A *coping pattern is a method used to deal with a common thread.* For example, overeating might be a coping pattern for dealing with anxiety and depression associated with an underlying issue of abandonment (common thread). Coping patterns are usually habitual. Coping patterns exist originally to avoid or defend against pain, anxiety, and other undesirable feelings and may increase pleasure. Thus, they are originally adaptive behaviors. They become ineffective when they are rigidly applied to all stressful situations or when they are no longer useful to the client.

For example, when a child is abused, dissociation can be a useful behavior for survival; however, later in life, this dissociation can become a barrier to interpersonal intimacy and the ability to live fully in the present moment. Most of the time, clients are not aware that they are using these coping mechanisms because these patterns have become ingrained in their unconscious. They don't even think about it; they just do it. It is very important for counselors to notice these patterns because clients do not recognize them on their own.

- **The Vicious Circle**

Every coping pattern carries with it a price to pay. The third part of basic case conceptualization requires you to map out how the client's coping patterns have created a vicious circle of emotional and social consequences that actually perpetuate the problem. No matter what clients do, they wind up in the same place.

The dissociated client most longs for intimacy; however, due to abuse, the client has learned to automatically dissociate when feeling stressed. So when the client feels the urge for intimacy, instead of searching for others (which would cause more anxiety and possible hurt) she automatically resorts to dissociation. She may remain mentally detached from the present for hours, leading to more isolation. Thus, a vicious cycle of longing for intimacy, dissociation, and isolation is solidified.

Another example might be stress at work: The presenting problem may be stress at work. The common thread may be an underlying feeling of not being appreciated in work, with family members, and with friends. The coping technique for that problem may be going out of his way to give more. And the vicious circle of over-extending oneself may result in bottled-up resentments and increased social withdrawal or isolation.

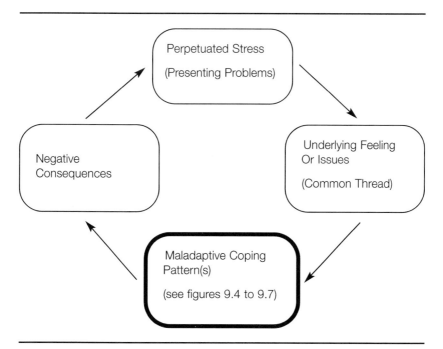

FIGURE 9.1.   Theme Analysis: Conceptualizing the Vicious Circle of Client Problem

Theme Analysis Example

Example 1

- **Common Thread: Powerlessness and Anxiety**

    Throughout the sessions, the client has spoken about situations where her husband often verbally abuses her when he gets home from work. This verbal abuse brings forth feelings of powerlessness and anxiety in the client.

- **Coping Pattern: Peace-making**

    Instead of confronting or discussing her emotional reactions with her husband, the client puts the blame on herself, their son, or her husband's job. She holds back her true, honest feelings in a quest for acceptance.

- **Vicious Circle: Stagnated Growth**

    The client's pattern of blaming herself is causing her pent-up frustration and stress. The high price of peace-making is her stagnated growth, to the point of low self-esteem and depression.

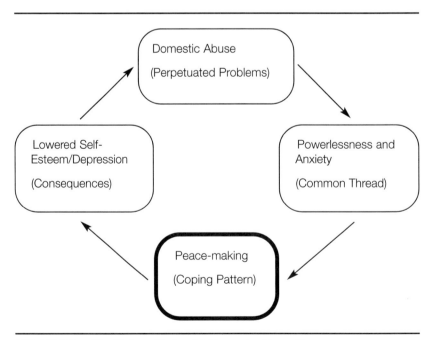

FIGURE 9.2.   The Vicious Circle of A Domestic Abuse Theme

Example 2

- **Common Thread: Perceived Injustice**

The client, named Tom, reports repeatedly the injustice that angers him and precipitates his fighting. He has brought up many instances of injustice where the perpetrators are the gangs, his neighbors (by their apathy), the alderman, the police, the realtor, his in-laws, and his family. He refers to his home as a "fortress," a haven of solitude against social onslaughts. He frequently refers to his forceful, volatile temper. Even close friends and his wife have been targets of it.

- **Coping Patterns**

Adopting a Rescuing Role

Tom's childhood leads him to feel discarded and unimportant. Without an effective male role model in his home, he resorted to fictional or idealized views of manhood and manliness. He has compensated for this weak self-concept and self-worth by creating a personal role as rescuer and hero. His actions seek to fulfill his ideal; yet he feels anachronistic in his milieu, creating numerous social and interpersonal conflicts. His thrill and excitement come in participating in and recounting his battles and rescues.

Heroic Fighting

Tom's fighting takes many particular forms: long-term banishment of his in-laws and his mother to hurt them for "wrongs," taunting gang members in the presence of police, rallying the troops by late-night phone-calling of neighbors to act, arguments and name-calling.

- **Vicious Circle: Perpetuated Sense of Being Devaluated**

Tom's devaluation by his family of origin leads to a weakened self-concept and self-worth. Without a male role model he sought one in fiction, and then sought to perform the protecting, defending, and rescuing obligations of a superhero. These rescuing actions lead him into conflict, and with conflict comes opposition. Opposition risks alienation, even when the opposition is justified (the client's gang fights.) Alienation serves as a reminder of injustice. This touches upon the childhood memory of his devaluation by family, thus perpetuating the cycle.

How Do Problems Originate and Perpetuate?

Problems begin from some ordinary life difficulty, of which there is never any shortage. This difficulty may stem from an unusual or fortuitous event. More often, the beginning is likely to be a common difficulty associated with one of the transitions regularly experienced in the course of life—marriage, the birth of a child, going to school, and so on. Most people handle such difficulties reasonably adequately—albeit that perfect handling is neither usual nor necessary—and thus you do not see them in your offices.

But for a difficulty to turn into a problem, only two conditions need to be fulfilled: (1) the difficulty is mishandled, and (2) when the difficulty is not resolved, more of the same ineffective solution is applied. Then the original difficulty escalates into a problem, whose eventual size and nature may have little apparent similarity to the original difficulty.

Thus, it is proposed that people's attempted "solutions," the very ways they are trying to alter a problem, contribute most to the problem's maintenance or exacerbation. These attempted but failed solutions include: (1) attempting to force something that can only occur spontaneously, (2) attempting to overcome a feared area by avoiding it, (3) attempting to be heard through opposition, (4) attempting to obtain compliance without asking for it directly, and (5) attempting to establish trust through defending oneself (Fisch, Weakland, and Segal, 1982).

If problem formation and maintenance are seen as parts of a vicious-circle process, then your primary aim need not be to resolve all difficulties, but to initiate a reversal. This means that implementing a small change in the vicious-circle interaction may initiate a beneficial-circle. Given this conception, you must be an active agent of change. Not only must you get a clear view of the problem behavior and the behaviors that function to maintain it, but also you must also consider what the most strategic small change in the "solutions" might be and take steps to instigate this change.

To generate a small change leading to the snowball effect of a beneficial circle in a client's life, you must first thoroughly understand how the vicious circle operates for each client. This is why it is so important to do the basic theme analysis, including finding common threads, coping patterns, and vicious circle impacts. You cannot really help the client initiate a breakthrough until you and the client both understand the behavioral pattern in the vicious circle.

How Does Change Happen?

Before you can help clients change their coping patterns, breaking the vicious circle, it is important to understand two things: First, do clients perceive the causes of their problem to be internal or external? Second, do they view the responsibility for problem resolution to be under their control (internal) or out of their control (external)? After you understand these two things about your clients, you can move them toward greater self-efficacy.

Self-efficacy (Bandura, 1982) refers to a client's sense of ability to mobilize whatever skills are needed to deal with the environment. Clients can increase their self-efficacy when counselors emphasize that (1) clients are responsible for solving the problem although they did not cause the problem, (2) clients' behaviors are within their own control, and (3) they themselves are capable of mastering their environment. Counselors who endorse this philosophy of helping tend to empower their clients to change.

But do you really believe that clients are responsible for solving their problems? That clients can control their behaviors? That they are capable of mastering their environment? The answers depend on which theoretical framework in counseling and psychotherapy you ascribe to. Basically, the helping orientation can be divided into four models (Brickman, Rabinowits, Karuza, Coates, Cohn, and Kidder, 1982) as shown in Figure 9. 3.

- The Moral Model: People are responsible both for creating and for solving their problems. In this model, the bad news is that, if you are depressed, you are the one who causes the depression, probably because you have a defect in your personality. And the dubious good news is that you must solve the depression by your internal power, probably through pulling yourself together or exercising better self-discipline.

- The Enlightenment Model: People are responsible for creating their problems but not for solving them. The bad news in this model is that you are

| | | (Cause of problem) | |
		Internal	External
(Responsibility for Problem Resolution)	Internal	Moral Model	Compensatory Model
		(Clients feel shamed, condemned, strained.)	(Clients feel liberated, empowered.)
	External	Enlightenment Model	Medical Model
		(Clients feel guilty, powerless.)	(Clients remain irresponsible and feel handicapped.)

FIGURE 9.3.   The four models of the helping orientation

the one who causes your depression, maybe due to some personality defect or sin. More bad news is that you cannot solve your depression, no matter how you sacrifice yourself. You must rely on an external power, such as God, Buddha, physicians, or psychiatrists, to solve the depression. This is the you-mess-it-up-and-you-better-put-yourself-in-someone-else's-hands-and-someone-will-come-to-show-the-way model.

- The Medical Model: People are responsible neither for creating their problems nor for solving them. In this model, the good news is that your depression is not your fault, the bad news is that you cannot fix it yourself. More likely, your depression is caused by a bio-chemical imbalance, and only a psychiatrist can help eliminate it by prescribing medication. This is the dependency model and requires good luck and a good health plan.

- The Compensatory Model: People are not responsible for creating their problems but are responsible for solving them. The good news, in this model, is that your depression is not your own creation, and is therefore not your fault. It is probably caused by family or by interpersonal environment, or by a bio-chemical imbalance. And another piece of good news is that you are able and responsible to solve your depression, mostly through psychotherapy, lifestyle changes, or making healthy decisions regarding relationships.

Among the four models, which one approximates the reality of human suffering? One way to conceptualize the suffering of human beings is through an equation formulated by George Albee (NMHA, 1986, p. 13):

$$\text{Incidence} = \frac{\text{Organic Factors} + \text{Stress} + \text{Exploitation}}{\text{Coping Skills} + \text{Self-esteem} + \text{Social Support}}$$

In this formula, the probability of mental distress equates to the amount of stressors that one experiences over the person's resources. If the person's stress level (organic factors, stress, and exploitation) are high and the resources (coping skills, self-esteem, and social support) are low, mental distress is ensured. Conversely, if a person has low stress and abundant resources, mental distress is unlikely. However, if a person's stress level is high but the resources are strong, that person will probably not develop mental problems. Finally, a person who has low stress and low resources is likely to get by OK until some traumas occur. It is only a matter of time.

In short, according to this model, mental health conditions (such as depression) result from overwhelming external life circumstances and lack of internal coping resources.

The compensatory model comes close to Albee's conceptualization. It emphasizes (1) problem externalization and (2) coping. Problem externalization frees clients' energy from shame and guilt and thus they can direct their energy outward to work on solving the problem. They feel liberated. The emphasis on coping patterns states that clients are not responsible for creating their problems, but their old coping patterns (see "Theme Analysis" earlier in this chapter) may have contributed to maintaining the problem. So clients are held responsible for changing their behavioral coping pattern, learning new coping skills, and building support systems. These factors are usually within a client's control and a client who learns to control them breaks through the vicious cycle that perpetuates the problem. Clients who are engaged in coping action usually feel empowered. When clients feel empowered, change occurs.

What Coping Patterns Should Be Changed?

Any coping patterns that do not help clients deal effectively with their everyday interactions in life should be changed. Coping techniques are strategies that people adopt to cope with difficult situations or intense, painful feelings. All people develop coping techniques early in life to adjust to life's hardships. Some coping techniques are adaptive and effective. Other coping techniques become maladaptive and self-defeating when they have become ingrained. You should honor clients' coping techniques; but you need to examine them to see whether they are still effective in your clients' adult lives. Some coping techniques serve clients well in their early lives, but are doing them a disservice in their adulthood. They prevent clients from living or feeling fully, and introduce difficulty into their interpersonal relationships. These ineffective coping patterns need to be changed.

For example, according to Yalom (1985, 1995), you cannot treat depression or any mental health condition *per se* because depression is the resulting symptom of life stressors and interpersonal interaction patterns. Rather, depression needs to be translated into interpersonal terms. With that translation, you can treat the underlying interpersonal coping patterns. For example, you can translate depression into coping styles characterized by suppressing anger, forming unrealistic expectations, allowing others to take one for granted, anticipating abandonment from others, not speaking up for oneself, and so on. When these coping patterns change into more active personal agency, then the client's ability to deal with life stressors will increase, leading to the ultimate elimination of the symptom (depression) and improved quality of life. This view about change is at sharp contrast with the medical model, which treats the symptom (such as depression) as an ultimate entity.

How can you tell whether a coping technique is adaptive or self-defeating? Trace the social and emotional consequences of these techniques.

Examine the vicious circle that a coping technique may be a part of (see "Theme Analysis" earlier in this chapter). Those coping patterns that are not helpful to the clients should be targets for intervention.

The following four charts, Figures 9.4, 9.5, 9.6 and 9.7 give examples of ineffective coping techniques that people use to deal with life's discomfort. Therapists should become aware of these coping techniques and try to determine the underlying circular consequences supported by the coping patterns. The four charts encompass internal coping mechanisms, external coping mechanisms, the mechanisms of minimizing, and the mechanisms of disowning.

More specifically, internal coping mechanisms are the *cognitive* techniques employed by the client. External coping mechanisms are the *behavior* patterns that others can observe. The mechanisms of minimizing are ways to *downplay* the problem itself but that paradoxically perpetuate the problem. And the mechanisms of disowning allow a person to avoid owning up to the reality of the problems either by blaming external sources or by blaming disassociated parts of themselves.

CONTEXTUAL ANALYSIS: INTERMEDIATE CASE CONCEPTUALIZATION

In the basic case conceptualization that occurs in the initial stage of counseling, you use theme analysis to identify the vicious circles that bind your

---

— Comparing the self to others (Everybody is . . . than I am)
— Forming unrealistic expectations (I should be able to . . .)
— Anticipating negative results (There is no hope for this . . .)
— Holding back honest feelings (I am great, really)
— Distorting feedback (You are just telling me that . . .)
— Creating false limitation (I can't . . . I can't . . .)
— Blaming oneself or others (I should have known better . . .)
— Imposing guilt on the self or others (You should have thought of it before . . .)
— Reviewing past hurts (I can never love again because . . .)
— Labeling the self or others (I am such an idiot . . .)
— Blanking one's mind (I cannot think of it anymore now . . .)
— Fantasizing (If only . . .)
— Intellectualizing (There must be a reason . . .)
— Selective forgetting (I can't remember . . .)
— Magnifying real problems (It is just too hard . . .)
— Rationalizing (I have to . . . because . . .)

FIGURE 9.4.   Internal Coping Mechanisms

— Attacking others, verbally or physically
— Throwing temper tantrums
— Manipulating others
— Laughing when it is not appropriate
— Being late for appointments
— Arguing for the sake of arguing
— Withholding sexuality in loving relationships
— Pouting
— Analyzing problems or situations when action is required
— Acting rashly in situations where thoughtful analysis is required
— "Nervous" tics or habits
— Failing to meet obligations
— Engaging in promiscuous or unloving sexual acts
— Lying
— Making sarcastic remarks
— Crying at inappropriate times
— Drinking too much
— Spending money beyond one's means
— Racial or religious bigotry
— Using drugs
— Smoking or chewing tobacco

FIGURE 9.5.   External Coping Mechanisms

— Ignoring	— Being chronically "busy"
— Comparing	— Nihilizing
— Joking	— Making others pay
— Numbing	— Therapizing
— Martyring	— Adapting

FIGURE 9.6.   Minimizing Techniques

— Blaming other people
— Fragmenting the mind and body
— Capitalizing on social, political, or economic inequities
— Embracing fatalistic conclusions

FIGURE 9.7.   Disowning Techniques

The above coping techniques (Figures 9.4, 9.5, 9.6, and 9.7) are extracted from Cudney and Hardy (1991) *Self-Defeating Behaviors.* New York: HarperCollins. pp 187-190. Reprinted by permission of HarperCollins Publishers, Inc.

clients. Next, in the middle stage of counseling, you examine the bigger picture. This task can be achieved by exercising intermediate case conceptualization — the contextual analysis. This exercise helps you see clients' problems from a broader framework, so that you can take into consideration the extenuating circumstances that perpetuate a client's problem.

Considering Contextual Factors

Specifically, intermediate case conceptualization consists of (1) revising and updating theme analysis and (2) analyzing factors that cause the client to develop ineffective coping patterns. First, why do you need an updated theme analysis? With time and new information, your concept about a client's problems and its supporting system will change. It is necessary to update your conceptualization of themes and also look for new insights into clients' issues.

Second, what are contextual factors? These are the factors that sustain clients' behavior patterns, often causing them to become exacerbated. These factors may include clients' prior life learning and external factors in society or the current environment.

● Prior Learning

Prior learning is the experience that predisposes the client to respond to stressors in a patterned way. Analyzing this prior learning leads you into clients' past histories, so that you can understand their problems from a more longitudinal context.

● Factors in Society or the Current Environment

Certain external forces, including the current living conditions and political circumstances, produce stress in clients' lives, enlisting them to respond in the patterned way.

Contextual Analysis Examples

The following examples illustrate how a client's prior learning and his or her extenuating circumstance contribute to current problems.

Example 1

In this case, the basic case conceptualization finds a consistent coping pattern of needing to please. After this pattern is identified, the therapist looks both at the client's prior learning and at factors in her current situations that propel her into a vicious cycle. This constitutes intermediate case conceptualization.

- **Prior Learning**

The client grew up in an alcoholic family where the father was an alcoholic and the mother was constantly hiding it from others. Her mother forbade the children to discuss the problem with outsiders. All the three children became perfect at covering up for their father. The client was the scapegoat in her family. Everyone used her. She was blamed for the problems in the family. She was the recipient of cruel pranks and jokes. Throughout her childhood and adulthood, the client found herself giving and wanting to please.

- **Factors in Society or the Current Environment**

In addition to her past history, the client's current domestic situation pulls her further into the pattern of pleasing. The client is a homemaker; her husband is the sole provider for the family. This creates a power imbalance, furthering her self-blame. The one-down position in her household recruits her to the pleasing behavior pattern.

Example 2

This is the case of Tom, whose coping pattern was observed in the basic case conceptualization (last section). His pattern was to defend and rescue others at the expense of his own safety.

- **Prior Leaning**

Tom experienced parental divorce when he was five. Both the court proceedings and the ensuing child support struggles over the years were filled with conflict. Tom's interaction with both parents over the years included verbal attacks and physical threats. As a young child, Tom felt powerless to resolve the fights and to maintain his family's equilibrium. However, at one point, with the support of his mother, Tom threatened to kill his father. He was rewarded for taking on the role as defender of his mother. His sense of power was increased when he was praised for coming to the defense of a niece after she was raped. The random schedule of these reinforcers sustained the "defender behavior."

- **Factors in Society or the Current Environment**

Tom tries to police his neighborhood from gang influences on his own. He has to defend the neighborhood because the local police are ineffective in dealing with the rampant crime in the area. In addition, the real estate agents in the area have allied to drive down real estate values, making profits for themselves. This environmental atmosphere creates more urgency for him to step into the spiraling danger and rescue the neighborhood and make it safer "for the children."

Note: The above example may sound absurd to you, but people who live in metropolitan areas (such as Chicago) understand the unfortunate reality of the situation.

UNIQUE-OUTCOME ANALYSIS: ADVANCED CASE CONCEPTUALIZATION

During the transition from the middle (awareness raising) to the later (problem resolution) stage of counseling, it is time to do the unique-outcome analysis. This exercise helps both the counselor and the client get out of the "problem-focused" mind set of the earlier stage of counseling. The therapeutic energy now can be devoted to the process of healing, which includes developing a new personal narrative.

A client often enters therapy with a story line about himself or herself full of problems. These problem-saturated stories omit other stories that are actually parts of the client's life. These omitted or censored stories usually feature the more competent and resourceful parts of the client. They are the gaps of the personal narrative. By exploring and discovering these gaps, you can help the client create a new personal narrative to achieve the therapeutic ends. In other words, a client entering therapy sees only the problems of the past; you collaborate with the client to create a new personal narrative—a narrative of a more complete picture, a narrative that reclaims the good.

Searching for the Unique Outcome

To move to the problem resolution stage of counseling, the case conceptualization focuses on unique-outcome analysis. What are unique outcomes? Unique outcomes are exceptions from the problem-dominated stories or the problem-saturated narratives. Unique outcomes can also be called *sparkling events*. They usually indicate a client's existing competence and resiliency. They existed already in the background but were unnoticed or forgotten by clients. They are the gaps.

These sparkling events can be identified and applied in the following three steps:

✔Exceptional Incidents
✔Alternative Meaning for Client
✔Positive Circular Effects

• Exceptional Incidents

The first part of a unique outcome is to identify clients' characteristics that are 180 degrees different from the themes or the problematic patterns that have been brought up in the previous sessions. These differences are virtues or strengths that clients usually do not acknowledge. Counselors should amplify the strengths so that they become the antidotes to clients' problems. What you strive to do is to uncover clients' hidden resources that may be used to break the previous vicious cycle.

- **Alternative Meaning for Client**

After you discover and amplify clients' hidden resources, the next step is to focus on identifying how these strengths have been used in the past. In other words, you reframe clients' motivations, causing them to see themselves in a more positive light.

- **Positive Circular Effects**

After clients see their behaviors in a more positive light, their self-esteem increases. As a result, their interaction with other people becomes more positive. This breaks the vicious cycle, creating a positive feedback loop.

Unique Outcome Analysis Example

This is the case of Tom again. In this analysis, the therapist searches for Tom's previously omitted competence and resiliency to fill up the gaps in his originally problem-focused story.

Exceptional Incidents

Deep capacity for caring

Tom's powerful and often productive love for his wife is apparent. He is proud of his support and encouragement while she completed her Master's degree. He not only wants to take care of her, but also empowers her to launch her own career. Despite conflict during the first year of marriage, he was able to manage the differences and make it a good relationship. His nobility, his nurturing and his deep concern for his wife indicate that he has resources that can bring forth the desired changes in his behaviors.

Ability to forgive injustices and make peace

After almost three years of major conflict and estrangement from his wife's parents, Tom now has reached a peaceful, even enjoyable relationship with his mother-in-law. He even looks toward the day when he can be her caretaker. There was a mutual relinquishing of grudges and anger. This demonstrates the client's ability to forgive injustices and make peace.

Alternative Meaning for Clients

The therapist's effort to emphasize Tom's caring and deep concern for his wife has renewed his self-identity as a loving and strong person. His ability to reach a peaceful relationship with his mother-in-law also led Tom to realize that he has the ability to forgive injustices and facilitate peace.

Positive Circular Effects

When Tom experiences conflict resolution, he experiences a peaceful state of mind. During those times, he enjoys activities and relationships more, both with his wife and with her family. As fighting subsides and he and his wife construct a more solid dyadic family, this fulfills his longing for the unified family he did not have in childhood. From her love and their solidified relationship he gains a stronger sense of value, accomplishment, and self-worth. As Tom feels more valued for who he is, and feels freed from his rescuing responsibilities, he may abandon his crusades and abate marital conflicts.

PREFERRED OUTCOMES ANALYSIS: THE FINAL CASE CONCEPTUALIZATION

The last stage of counseling focuses on helping clients consolidate their newly developing self-identities. This helps clients to avoid relapse into former vicious circles. To achieve this, you use preferred outcome analysis to direct the sessions with them. What are preferred outcomes? Preferred outcomes are the client's possible self. They are the preferred images or preferred behaviors that the client wishes to envision in his or her daily life. The difference between a unique outcome and a preferred outcome is that unique outcome is the existing yet forgotten competence, whereas a preferred outcome is the client's potential not yet developed. Therapists can plant the seeds of these preferred outcomes in the client's mind to help the client realize that potential.

Planting the Seeds of Preferred Outcomes

Therapists can plant seeds of successful change in clients by helping them focus on their envisioned future, including:

- ✔Envisioned Competency Areas
- ✔Envisioned Self-Identity
- ✔Envisioned Relationship Styles

● **Envisioned Competency Areas**

Since the client has developed a new narrative, your task now is to help the client envision those newly rediscovered resources to be used in the future. For example, if the client has constructed a new narrative with herself as a person who has acted courageously in the past, then the client can be led to envision how a new life would look using that trait of courage. If a client can envision success, it will come.

● **Envisioned Self-Identity**

The therapist directs clients to construct new beliefs about themselves including their purposes in life, their self-worth, their meaning in life, and what makes each of them a unique person.

● **Envisioned Relationship Styles**

The therapist directs clients to form ideas about how their relationships will be more fulfilling and more meaningful.

Preferred Outcome Analysis Example

This is still the case of Tom.

Envisioned Competency Areas

Tom has begun to envision peaceful times as active and fulfilling, rather than "neutral." He started to entertain the idea that confrontation with problems does not necessitate a fight. He may practice some basic mediation skills and brainstorm less dangerous alternatives that serve the same end, and make a plan of personal action for future gang occurrences. He can foresee choosing the path of least physical danger in order to spare his wife the stress.

Tom expresses interest in using the two-chair technique (see Chapter 7) to explore his unfinished business with his estranged mother. This can lead him into deeper awareness of her continuing influence over his current choices. In that way, he can perhaps better own his coping patterns and come to explore his preferred way of living.

Envisioned Self-Identity

Tom is beginning to envision his own identity evolving from a defender toward a facilitator. He is allocating more of the responsibilities for block organization to other neighbors. He is listening to the ideas of his neighbors and helping them implement their ideas: a park patrol, a telephone tree, a neighborhood clean-up weekend, social gatherings, and so on. He is providing them with some of the contacts and resources he has in law enforcement. He is gaining a greater sense of pride that others are building upon what he started, with a larger support network for neighborhood safety. As a result, he finds that he spends less time on block projects, but is getting more done to achieve his goals.

Envisioned Relationship Styles

Tom is starting to picture that taking care of his immediate family is more important than caring for the whole neighborhood. He has let time help him forgive some grudges, especially against his wife's family. He is beginning to think of safer places to move with her in the future, and he is hoping to own his home. He is starting to see that mediation takes more courage and more intelligence than just "going out there and getting my hands dirty in a fight!"

He wants to work on recognizing the sources of his anger. He is now more aware of the hurt behind his anger. He is willing to work towards a less combative, more imperturbable relationship with those at odds with his values.

HOW TO WRITE CASE NOTES

All counseling agencies require counselors to keep progress notes after each counseling session, although private practitioners may prefer to keep notes in different ways. Because the progress notes can be supenoed in a court case, the language used in these cases needs to be carefully chosen. These notes should state the facts, and not include therapists' speculations or judgment.

Following are two formats for case notes: (1) SOAP format, and (2) the narrative format.

SOAP Case Notes

SOAP is the acronym for Subjective, Objective, Assessment, and Plan. More specifically, the "Subjective" part documents what the client says is happening or *the presenting problem* as the client reports it. The "Objective" part documents the counselor's observations of the client's affect, non-verbal behaviors, appearance, or mental status in the session, not outside the session. The "Assessment" part records the counselor's understanding of the client's core issues, themes, or behavioral patterns; client strengths and resources; the client's preferred alternative self-narrative, evaluation of progress to date; and notation of any additional information needed. This assessment section may appear as the summary of the theme analysis. The assessment should be as objective as possible without emphasizing underlying pathology.

Finally, the "Plan" part documents the client's plan to achieve treatment goals or eliminate identified problems. The "Plan" part may also include the counselor's plans to improve the working alliance or trust and the client's feeling of being heard or validated, to increase client self-awareness of behavior patterns, discrepancy, and forgotten strengths/resources, and to increase the client's sense of competence and self-efficacy.

Example

- Subjective: Tom reported instances of injustices around him and the fights that have resulted. He said that he is becoming more aware of the emotional impact that his actions are having upon his wife. Although he reported that there is no problem with his wife, he chose to discuss the issues with his wife for the entire session.

- Objective: Tom showed little change in his vocal or physical non-verbal cues. He remained controlled, rational, passive and inanimate. However, when the counselor role-played his wife begging him to move, he paused, his voice lowered and quavered, he sighed, his volume lowered and his tone softened. Yet when his choices were explored, his voice again became flat. The exception to this was that when he was confronted with inconsistencies, he stammered, stuttered, and his pitch raised. He also avoided direct eye contact, looking at the wall rather than the counselor.

- Assessment: Tom's conflict with his wife seems to be rooted in his early life which was filled with familial chaos and conflict. He coped with this chaos and conflict by denying his emotions, keeping them at a distance. His strength is that he has a strong sense of morality and justice, and has high ideals for a better environment. However, to reach his ideal, he both literally and mentally struggles and fights. This perpetuates chaos and conflict, yet paradoxically fosters his sense of power, strength, and esteem. Through his actions and the heroic role, he gains a sense of leadership, importance and worth. His actions place him and his wife in emotional and physical jeopardy. So he risks losing his life and his wife. He claims to be growing tired of the responsibility he has assumed and says he cares about his wife's stress about his fighting, but he does not know how to change.

- Plan: Although this session focuses mainly on his conflict with his wife, there are still other areas of conflict that need to be discussed: (1) conflict with neighbors, (2) conflict with in-laws; and (3) conflict with mother. In the next session, Tom wished to focus on his conflict with his mother.

Tom has cut off communication with her to avoid direct conflict which perpetuates the hurt he feels. Exploration of his feelings about his mother may help Tom resolve other areas of conflict in his life.

Narrative Case Notes

A narrative case note provides an overview of what has transpired in the session from the counselor's point of view. It generally follows the chronology of the session, although themes or topics may be treated discretely.

Example

Tom appeared angry and distracted at the start of the session. He was initially difficult to engage. He described a conflict with his wife and fears losing her. He seems to feel better after devising a plan to resolve conflict with his wife. He plans to gain insight into his interpersonal pattern by exploring his conflict with his mother in the future session.

APPENDIX A

TRAINEE SESSION SAMPLES

The following session samples are drawn from the work materials of those trainees who, for the first time in their lives, are learning how to counsel clients. These are their initial counseling experiences using the skills and techniques they learned from this book. The clients they work with are either peer clients or outside clients. The sessions in these samples are from the early stages of the counseling process.

Sample I

This is the transcript of a third lab session in an individual counseling skill training class. Stina, the student counselor, practiced peer counseling with Betty, the student client. Both parties' identities are masked to keep confidentiality. Permission from the client was obtained.

Counselor: **Betty, nice to see you again.**

Client: Nice to see you, Stina.

Counselor: **I know that making this appointment is often difficult; let's work toward making this a rewarding session. (A pause.) We've been exploring your anger and the effects the anger has on your life. Mostly we concentrated on the school situation in which you communicated your disappointment through an outburst of anger and overeating (summarization).**

Client: Yeah, overeating is a way of letting out my anger.

Counselor: **How do you feel about it personally (probing)?**

Client: I think I feel inadequate.

Counselor: **Hum . . . (minimum encourager).**

Client: In many situations when I am angry I feel I am old enough and should be able to do certain things that I am not able to do and I end up getting very angry because I don't know what to do. This is in the job situation. In my personal life I hide my anger: I overeat.

Counselor: **Sounds like you deal with anger and sense of inadequacy with eating. You mentioned you felt exercise has been a positive coping technique for you. How does that work (reflection of feelings + probing)?**

Client: I might use the rowing machine to be the person I am angry with.

Counselor: **Um-hum . . .**

Client: If I can beat the machine, by doing whatever exercise, it can relieve some frustrations, because when I am so focused I don't think about anything and my whole head gets cleared. So, this is the only exception: when I do this particular exercise, I feel a lot of relief.

Counselor: **Okay. So exercising has shown two positive benefits for you: It relieves your mind and gives you a chance to get rid of the pain so you have a moment of cooling peace.** (The client says "Right!") **If you cannot get rid of the anger you almost use it as a punching bag.** (The client: "Yes!") **Your exercise can be almost cathartic.** (The client: "Yes!") **How often are you exercising right now (summarization + probing)?**

Client: Well, I had been exercising two times a week, but I have been so bogged down with schoolwork, both graduate school and my teaching job— that I have not put forth any effort at all. I can already feel differences in my body.

Counselor: **Has your anger or frustration level been higher (closed probing)?**

Client: It was until summer session. Though I am angry or frustrated with certain students and their behavior, I think I am more laid back because there are two other people to talk to the students besides me so I can be the teacher and leader and not have to deal with students' disruptive behaviors. That makes a difference.

Counselor: **We have talked about your anger at work mostly. Let's talk a little bit about how the anger influences you. Can you tell me how it makes you feel about yourself when you are angry (clarifying statement)?**

Client: I feel like I have given the person every opportunity to change whatever behavior I would like them to change. I am so frustrated with them not changing that. I start seeing red; I just want to scream out and I do scream in some situations, put down others, like "Your mamma's on drugs. That's why you act like this." I don't know how to describe what it is. I guess I get a bright red hot feeling!!

Counselor: **It sounds as if you are describing a heated situation where you feel your temperature almost bubbling to a boil,** (the client: "Right!") **and just about to erupt. That makes you come out with sarcastic comments. . . (advanced empathy: vivid language).**

Client: I come out with sarcastic comments and I do that as opposed to doing something violent. I can see how, in some situations, I could get to the point when behavior is so repetitive on the other person's part that I could shake them, hit them, punch them, or do something physical. So the sarcastic remarks prevent me from doing that. In other words, I use the sarcastic remarks to prevent physical contact with the other person.

Counselor: **Hum. So it actually is a saving tool for you, a saving tool from doing something much more violent. You have used put-downs to hold your reins back from the temptation of physical abuse. Although it is not the most preferred method of coping, but you have found it to be a method that holds you back from doing something that is worse (advanced empathy: growth edge).**

Client: Right!

Counselor: **And I sense that you are almost saying that you would like to find something better than sarcasm (advanced empathy).**

Client: Yes, I would like not to allow other people's behavior to bother me and I would like to be able to own up to my anger in my personal life.

Counselor: **How do you feel about your anger (probing)?**

Client: I don't like how I am when I am angry. Like last night, I was in the same situation. I have a friend I have been friends with for twenty years, and she has been delaying taking me out for my birthday. My birthday was in August. We finally got around to going out last night. There was a discrepancy over time—she wanted to take me out at 6:30. Well, I am a diabetic and I have to eat at specific times. I did ask... I was strong enough to ask for a sightly earlier time as a compromise. But it was not quite as early. I knew that getting to her house at 6:30 we would not be eating until 8:00, and that is detrimental to my health in the first place—I cannot eat that late!! I was trying to get any earlier time so I could eat earlier and then have a longer time in which to, ah, visit. In other words my body needs a longer time to . . . ah, I cannot eat late.

Counselor: **Sounds like you are saying the situation frustrated you on two levels. First, she is very late at giving you a birthday party, and that hurts you (reflection of feeling).**

Client: Yes, that was a hurt!

Counselor: **Second, it hurts that she does not recognize you are a diabetic. Most people know diabetics need to eat on a regimented schedule. You feel that if she cared about you she would have known you have to eat early. And it angered you that you had to put your foot down (reflection of feeling).**

Client: But see, that's part of my problem. I don't speak up. I couldn't speak up with her.

Counselor: **It sounds like you did make a compromise, yet you have made some steps. You recognized your anger and almost said, "Hey, wait a minute, I have got to eat earlier" (advanced empathy: growth edge).**

Client: But see, I did not even do that. I just asked if we could move it earlier, so I just compromised. But again it's me compromising! (said with anger) Me being the good guy, me not expressing that I was angry. Because, again, if I am angry again I am going to lose the person I want to be with.

Counselor: **Um hum.**

Client: That is a big fear of mine!

Counselor: **You fear that if you stand up for yourself, you will be isolated** (Client: "Right!") **and you will not have a friend and they will not be there for you.** (Client: "Right! Right!") **So learning to express your feelings adequately is very important to you (advanced empathy + reflection of meaning).**

Client: I want to learn how to properly express my anger.

Counselor: **How often are you afraid to say something to your friends (probing)?**

Client: I am always worried!!

Counselor: **You are afraid that if you say something wrong to your friends, they will leave you all alone (reflection of feeling).**

Client: I guess I am always afraid I am going to lose the person.

Counselor: **That must be scary** (reflection of feeling).

Client: It is scary. I guess feelings of abandonment ran through my life for a long time.

Counselor: **You mentioned your dad and your mom were gone when you were very little (paraphrasing).**

Client: Right!

Counselor: **That had to be very difficult. How are you feeling now (focusing)?**

Client: I still fear that feeling of abandonment. I feel alone, isolated. I don't have an immediate family. I am afraid to confront anybody for fear that they will leave me.

Counselor: **Although you grew up alone, you've done a number of things really well for yourself, You have managed to maintain a job for a long time—which is difficult for many people. You have friendships and positive things that have remained stable. Yet, some of the things you have done to maintain your stability have led you to lose a little of yourself. To avoid being alone, you end up compromising yourself (advanced empathy + confrontation).**

Client: You bet!! You bet!! To avoid being alone I compromise myself. Yet, there are still so many times I feel isolated and alone, so many times I feel there is no one there for me.

Counselor: **It hurts so much to compromise and yet still be so alone (reflection of feeling).**

Client: Yeah . . . (Client's eyes were tearing. Counselor found Kleenex for her. And the lab time was running out.)

Counselor: **Our time is running out. Before we leave I want to share with you my respect for you. You have made a lot of strides here today. Sometimes in the counseling process steps forward are difficult and they hurt. They bring things to the surface, things we don't want to remember or recognize (counselor self-disclosure: professional reassurance). We started to do this here today, together we started to see some things that are real issues—not just behavior problem and situations. You are doing very hard work here, and you are on the right track. I am proud of your courage to do this hard work (feedback giving: affirmative feedback). I am looking forward to continuing working with you next week.**

Client: See you next week. (Client left in reflective mode.)

Sample Two

This is a first session with an outside client. Transcription was permitted by the client. Client's identity is protected.

Counselor: **Thank you for coming in. We only have about a half hour together. This might be a chance for you to talk about things that are concerning you and to make things a little more clear about how to approach these issues. Is there anything that's on your mind today (role induction + probing)?**

Client: A couple of things. One is really the future, the job I have now. Do I want to stay there? Now that I'm married, I have to think about supporting my wife, but I kind of want to do something different. The other thing is my Mom and Dad. They're getting older and just the responsibility of taking care of that. I wonder if they'll need to come live with us.

Counselor: **I'm hearing two concerns. The first is the concern about the future, career wise, is that right (perception checking)?**

Client: Yes.

Counselor: **. . . and the other is about your family, particularly how you will care for your parents now that they are getting older (paraphrasing).**

Client: Right, yeah, they're getting older, they're in their sixties, and I wonder whether I should be preparing now to have them stay in a nursing home or maybe have them live with us but we're thinking of moving into a smaller place. I wonder if I'll be ostracizing my parents if I do that.

Counselor: **So you've been thinking of making changes, but I sense that there's somewhat a fear that you're deserting your parents (reflection of feeling).**

Client: Right, they always enjoy coming up here and everything and also as I approach the age of 40, I wonder if I might be going through something. Like the plans I've made, maybe I'm not meeting the expectations I laid out for myself. Then you throw in the uncertainty of their failing health, and it causes me concern.

Counselor: **Among the issue with your career, the concerns about your parents, and the desire to more fully meet your goals and expectations. I wonder which of these concerns you the most at this moment (focusing)?**

Client: Um . . . I would say the future of my career. Since I've been doing that job for 15 years, do I want to do the same thing for the next 15 or do something else? And if I am doing something else, would it be enough to support my family? Would doing something else be selfish, and not taking into consideration the wife and kids?

Counselor: **So you'd be willing to take more risks, but you're married and you have to look at the bigger picture (reflection of meaning).**

Client: Yeah, right. And the thing is, when you're single, all you have to think about is yourself And being single for so long I wonder why I didn't make that decision when I was single. What held me back? And why would I want to do it now that I'm married as opposed to when I was single?

Counselor: **When you ask yourself that, what kind of answers do you come up with (probing)?**

Client: Uh . . . One was maybe the fear of doing something different . . . but then I go back to just after college when I really enjoyed working with my hands, but here I am working in an office. I think that maybe it's just because I'm frustrated with my job that I'm thinking this way. With all the expectations and hours I'm working, I think I'd enjoy it a lot more if I just worked with my hands . . . though I'm not that good at working with my hands.

Counselor: **I hear a sense of frustration (reflection of feeling).**

Client: Yeah, that's it. I would say frustration more than fear.

Counselor: **Fear (minimum encourager).**

Client: Yeah, fear of change. I'm the type of person that doesn't change very easily. I've been living in the same house for 10 years, I plan to be married to the same woman for the next 30 years, or more. All the things in my life usually have continuity to them. So maybe that fear of change holds me back from experiencing more things because I feel I won't meet the expectations that are within me.

Counselor: **You talk about being resistant to change, but I notice that you also talk about a lot of changes you've recently undergone. You're recently married, you're planning to move, and you've had some changes at your career as well (advanced empathy: growth edge).**

Client: Right, and all of those were more... Well, the fear of marriage was minimal—that I knew was the right thing to do. With moving, I hesitated because I really liked the area I was living in though I'm now looking forward to it. With work, it had to do with a promotion. So, when I look at those changes, they didn't really have much fear in them.

Counselor: **So you went through those changes, and are still a part of them. Do you feel you have a tendency to place high expectations on yourself (paraphrasing + probing)?**

Client: I would say I didn't face up to that, but it's there. When I look at my family and my wife, they accept me. I guess within me I feel that there's certain things I feel I can achieve, and if I'm not, I'm disappointed. And the thing is, is it an activity I should be accomplishing? Or is it a way of life? If it's an activity, and I pursue it, but after I achieve it find the satisfaction isn't there, what then?

Counselor: **So your fear of change is due to your fear of being disappointed (reflection of feeling).**

Client: Yeah, maybe I don't handle disappointment well. Maybe because I don't want to disappoint people. And if I feel I've disappointed people—someone told me I'm a people-pleaser—and if I try to always please people instead of just doing it. I don't know. See—you're caught in between because you want to please people, but . . .

Counselor: **When you said someone had told you that you are a people-pleaser, you smiled. But I can hear from your voice that you're not satisfied with that. How would you describe the real feeling behind that smile (immediacy + advanced empathy + probing)?**

Client: I like pleasing people. That's who I am and it brings me joy to do that. The thing is, if I do it too much I exclude my wife. She has to be first.

Counselor: **You run into situations where you want to please everybody, but end up not pleasing those you love the most (paraphrasing).**

Client: Right.

Counselor: **How do you see the people-pleasing related to your uncertainty regarding your future (probing)?**

Client: That's a big component, but I think I really feel the most important thing is the happiness of it. I look at decisions I've made in the past, and it's worked out. Like when I got advice from my dad about my first job out of college. If he didn't give me support, I probably wouldn't have done it. That's more getting advice than people-pleasing, though. When I look at the future, I look more at the happiness of the job I'm doing.

Counselor: **So you place happiness on the job as a very high priority (reflection of meaning).**

Client: Yes, for the amount of hours I'm at the job, if I'm not happy, I should be doing a different thing. My job goes well until I start having to travel, then it's a diminishing effect. I'm away from my family, and I wonder if I should quit the job because of it, or maybe get a different job within the company. But the fear of that . . . So what do I do? Maybe nothing.

Counselor: **You feel paralyzed (reflection of feeling).**

Client: Yes, paralyzed.

Counselor: **I get the feeling that at one time you really liked your job, but some changes have come about, especially in regard to travel, that have left you dissatisfied (advanced empathy).**

Client: When I was younger, I really enjoyed it, but now that I'm married, I'd rather be spending time with my wife. And when I'm in a hotel room by myself, I realize that this would have been the time that I would have been spending with my wife, and it seems like I'm working overtime. It causes disappointment; you're probably right on that.

Counselor: **You mentioned before that you wondered whether your career should be an occupation or a lifestyle. It seems like you have a good idea of what an ideal lifestyle would be for you. What would that look like for you (paraphrasing + probing)?**

Client: That's a good question. The ideal lifestyle would let me work with other people, but also by myself at times. Also, I like projects, where you have a beginning and end, where it takes a long period of time. If I had a project that took three years, I'd enjoy that. Those two factors, but most importantly is teamwork. I don't know if this is a dichotomy, but if I can work on my own and others work on their own, then bring together what we've worked on, I feel that's teamwork. Everyone coming together in the end would carry a big bonanza for me.

Counselor: **In a sense, you like working alone, but also as part of a team. Are you not having a chance to do that at your current position (paraphrasing + probing)?**

Client: We've had a large turnover in the last year, but before that there were a lot of people with negative attitudes. I don't handle negative attitudes very well, and so it took a lot of fun out of it for me. I disassociated from them. It's getting better now, though, and I wonder if it was really the people and not the travel that made me dissatisfied. I'm enjoying it more.

Counselor: **I hear you saying that the travel isn't the whole issue, but it's the people (paraphrasing).**

Client: Yeah. I don't handle negative people very well. There's too much to life to complain all the time. Yet here I am paralyzed and not really acting satisfied.

Counselor: **Again, you smile, but I sense disappointment (advanced empathy).**

Client: Yeah, sometimes you know what to do, but being a people-pleaser, maybe it's easier to please positive people. I feed off of their affirmation. I guess I'm thinking that the dissatisfaction will pass as it has in the past.

Counselor: **We've talked about a number of things, all related to the career, with a common thread involved. You want to feel happy in your job but** you want to spend time with your family. Underneath it all is a real desire to help others, but sometimes you get caught up in trying too hard to please others (advanced empathy: identifying theme + reflection of meaning).

Client: Yeah, right.

Counselor: **You also talked about being afraid of making changes because you are afraid of the disappointment. I'm curious as to whom you feel you'd be disappointing (clarifying statement).**

Client: Myself.

Counselor: **It goes back to placing high expectations on yourself (advanced empathy).**

Client: Yes, my wife would support me, but I wonder if I switched to doing something with my hands, that I'd think I was wasting my abilities. Am I really doing what I'm capable of doing, and if I'm not I'd get disillusioned in a couple of years. By then, I might have lost the current knowledge to do what I'm doing now.

Counselor: **You feel like you could make a change, but it wouldn't satisfy you in the long run to work below your potential, and that you might be burning bridges (advanced empathy).**

Client: Exactly, right.

Counselor: **You talk about being a people pleaser. Yet, when you talk about who you are afraid of disappointing, you say yourself. How do you make sense of that (confrontation: discrepancy)?**

Client: I think I please people in regard to activities, which I don't mind doing. But there's a certain part of me that goes to the core, and if someone wants me to do something against that, I'd say no, because I have to answer to myself. In the same way, it goes to the job. I guess I feel that within the bottom of me there's something that I should be doing in this world. Let me tell you, there are certain jobs which I've done outside of my career that just strike a chord with me, and I'm always thinking, "Why am I not doing this all the time?" And it's because other things came into play—the pay or whatever—but that one I can definitely say, if I really found such a job—boom, I'd be there. You can't put a price on that—that's who I am, and there'd be no more people-pleasing.

Counselor: **You're seeking more purpose (reflection of meaning).**

Client: Yeah, what is my purpose (client in reflective mode)? Is it to be a husband, to be a son? You spend so much time working, and it goes right to you.

Counselor: **When you started talking about things where you felt that purpose, you became very animated. You straightened up and began to use you hands. I wonder . . . What were some of those things (immediacy + probing)?**

Client: They were activities where I was working with people — doing construction work, totally foreign to what I do now. It was a project to build things that would benefit them. They were people outside of my own culture here, so it had the benefits of bridge building; it was something that was accomplished over a two- or three-year period. The most important thing was the relationships that were built as a result of the project.

Counselor: **And you don't feel that your current position allows you to do that (paraphrasing).**

Client: Not as deeply, because the things that I do now are not life-changing or life-affecting to the people I work with now.

Counselor: **So you want to make a difference (reflection of meaning).**

Client: Right, make a difference (client animated)!

Counselor: **We've talked about a number of issues, but they've all come back to the idea that you really desire to work in a job where you can help people and make a difference in their lives, and by doing so, you will gain a sense of purpose in your own life (advanced empathy: influencing summary).**

Client: Right.

Counselor: **Well, we're just about to run out of time, but I wonder if you'd consider doing something between now and next time if you have a chance, and that is to write down those things that you feel are holding you back from changing into a position where you're making a difference. Then, take those things one by one and consider how practical it would be to overcome them (homework assignment).**

Client: OK.

Counselor: **Take care! Have a good week!**

Client: Thank you. I appreciate it.

Sample 3

This is a second session with another outside client. Transcription was permitted by the client. The client's name was changed to protect identity.

Counselor: **I'd like to thank you for coming in today. We have about half an hour together. Let's make good use of this time. What would you like to start with (greeting + probing)?**

Client: As you know from last week, I am going through a divorce and it will be two years and one of the concerns I have is in the dating area. It's new for me. Based on past experiences, I'm not sure I know how to handle dating or what to expect. So, it's a whole new world for me and I'm probably going into it with mixed emotions and certain expectations. Right or wrong, I don't know which they are, so it's unknown territory for me.

Counselor: **So you haven't dated in a while and you are concerned about how to date again (paraphrasing).**

Client: Very much so, because I think I'm coming into it with . . . Well, uh, being married for 17 years, you are kind of programmed into doing things differently and now that you are out of that and into a more healthy mental attitude, you want to make sure that you don't make the same mistakes or fall into patterns that you are accustomed to from the past.

Counselor: **You are wondering whether your old ways of living and feeling during your marriage may resurface in your new dating experiences (paraphrasing).**

Client: Sure, sure, it's scary and because I don't want that to happen. I want things in a more healthy, more whole, more adult relationship than I was accustomed to and I don't know if I am going to be able to handle that or have that. So, it's a concern because it's a growing period for me.

Counselor: **When you say you don't know what's out there, I sense a real sound of doubt as your voice tapers off (advanced empathy).**

Client: It's new for me. It's not like I dated a lot of people before I got married. I've been married for 17 years and right up to that I dated my husband for eight years. So, all of this is new and I don't know where everybody is at.

Counselor: **Can you tell me something more about how it feels to think about going out and dating new men? How does that feel to you (focusing)?**

Client: It's scary because of my marriage, the experiences in my marriage.

Counselor: **What kind of experiences (probing)?**

Client: The abuse that I've encountered, the control factor, all of that is very scary to me, because now I don't have that anymore, which is great. So, now it's kind of getting out of a cage and being on your own and doing things with your own feelings and so I'm kind of trying all of this out. So, yes it's scary because it will either validate that my feelings are OK, on situations or expectations, or they are not. Or maybe I'm still going to find out that I'm still not ready for outside relationships.

Counselor: **You felt abused, neglected, and sometimes belittled in you marriage, and you are wondering if that is going to happen again (reflection of feelings).**

Client: Sure, will I pick the same type of men or will I be able to stand up for myself when I see these characteristics in somebody or will I be able to say no, that's not for me? Will I become needy, will I become co-dependent again?

Counselor: **Can you elaborate a little more on the parts of yourself that you would like to see more of (solution focused question: looking for unique outcome)?**

Client: I look forward to a future when I am free of the abuse and I'm free of the control. So, in that respect, I'm happy and I know what I don't want. So maybe the inner strength within me will say no, this is not good for me. But, I like the freedom—I can come and go as I please and that I relish.

Counselor: **Despite all you've been through, you have an excitement in you about the future (advanced empathy: growth edge).**

Client: I still have too much to go through and work out. But, even interacting with men, which I don't know how to do on a different level. So it's exciting in one sense because I will be able to try out new things and try out my feelings and be able to say what I want to say and not feel threatened. So, in that sense it is exciting.

Counselor: **I sense your desire to test out new grounds (advanced empathy: growth edge).**

Client: Yes, I want to feel healthy. I want to be able to identify abuse, be able to identify when a person is controlling, or be able to identify when a person is manipulative, and be able to set those boundaries and live by them. But, if I don't, then I know I still need time and I pull back and I know that I still need some help in that area because it is a new thing for me.

Counselor: **So, feeling healthy is a new thing for you, and feeling healthy means being able to identify abuse, being able to see it happening and being able to stand up and say no, you won't take it (reflection of meanings).**

Client: Yes, yes.

Counselor: **I notice you are rubbing your hands (immediacy).**

Client: Yes. It's kind of exciting because then, it's what you've been taught and then you are like a little child and now you are gonna go out and walk and test the grounds to see how good you do it. So, in that respect I am looking forward to it because I need it, I need it. I'm not gonna know if it's working if I don't use it in my mental attitude in men in general, I guess, because of my marriage and/or family and friends with boundaries. You know, I was always a pleaser and it's exciting for me to say that it's okay for me to say no. Whereas, at one time it was hard for me to say no or I could not say no.

Counselor: **Whereas in the past you found yourself unable to say no to your husband and certain family members, you now find yourself having the ability to say no. How does that make you feel personally (paraphrasing + focusing)?**

Client: It feels great, it feels very freeing, it feels that I am in control of my life instead of someone controlling me and it feels wonderful, just wonderful. I can't describe it.

Counselor: **I really appreciate all of the hard effort that you have put into your life by trying to overcome the feelings that you have had from your** divorce, the feelings that you've had about your husband and your family (counselor self-disclosure: professional reassurance).

Client: It hasn't been easy but it's something that I was fortunate in the fact that I became aware of it. So, I don't look at it as a bad thing anymore. At one time I did, I looked at it as a bad thing and with a lot of anger. But, I consider myself as being lucky that I am out of that relationship now. I keep telling myself that I still have a chance to do things the right way.

Counselor: **I see tears in your eyes as you say that (immediacy).**

Client: Because it's scary. It's scary on one hand but to be given another chance is great.

Counselor: **Let's try something. I would like you to turn your attention inward and focus on what you are feeling at this moment (directives).**

Client: I'm feeling pain because of what has happened. That pain will always be there, it's never gonna go away. But, I have to learn how to deal with it, which I do and move on. Because I don't forget it but I can forgive the person for the pain.

Counselor: **So, you feel your way to have a new beginning is to forgive him although you don't feel you can forget (reflection of feelings).**

Client: Right, I can forgive him but I can't forget. Obviously this did happen to me and it's a reminder of things that I don't want to happen to me.

Counselor: **Please specify what things you do not want to happen to you again (focusing).**

Client: I don't want the verbal abuse, the control, the manipulation. I want it my way, not anybody else's, but my way and according to what makes me feel good, not for somebody else's feelings.

Counselor: **You want to live for yourself (advanced empathy: growth edge).**

Client: Yes.

Counselor: **I appreciate your new found assertiveness of not wanting to be treated with abuse, neglect, and control (professional reassurance).**

Client: Right, and manipulation. So I am very fortunate that I am aware of the fact of what was happening even at this late age. There are many women whom I've spoken with who are aware of it but they just don't know what to do with it. Either they are too old or they just live with it. What else am I gonna do? So, I am fortunate in that area.

Counselor: **I notice you are looking down when you say that (immediacy).**

Client: Just kind of a sense of peace. Peace is very important to me because I have had turmoil all my life.

Counselor: **After all of the confusion and the overwhelming feelings that you've had for so many years, you are starting to feel uplifted and it sounds like you are starting to see the light (advanced empathy: growth edge).**

Client: I see the light, I just have to know how to get there and do it in a healthy and whole way. So, yes I see the light. I know where it is. I just have to make sure that I get there whole.

Counselor: **Can you elaborate and tell me how it would feel to be whole (focusing)?**

Client: How it would feel to be whole. I don't know, but I can only speculate that I would feel like I'd be radiating with light.

Counselor: **Your face lights up when you talk about the way you want to feel and the way you are starting to feel now (immediacy).**

Client: Yes, to me that's what it would be, this air of just shining sense of peace and radiance, that's what it would be. I look forward to it.

Counselor: **You feel that the feeling of enlightenment is going to be in the future (paraphrasing).**

Client: Yes, and now that I am in the position that I am in I can either fall back to the old patterns or be strong and go for the light. I am going for the light.

Counselor: **Despite all the things, you really have a lot of strength to move forward (advanced empathy).**

Client: I have to, I have to for me. I've had the dark side and now I want the light side.

Counselor: **When you talk about the dark side, you look like you are about to cry (immediacy).**

Client: Well, it was painful, that's how it was. It was dark, sad, painful, depressing, just gloom.

Counselor: **Even though you have had mental scars, you plan on moving forward and not letting it stop you (advanced empathy: growth edge).**

Client: In one respect I look forward to the whole future and in another respect I still tread lightly because it is scary and it is unknown territory. So, in that respect I'm scared. But, I want the light, I want that light.

Counselor: **Your voice sounds like you are slowly starting to emerge from your cocoon and reach for the light (advanced empathy).**

Client: Yes, I am looking forward to it and there are going to be bumps along the way. I'm not afraid of opening up new doors because of where I've come from.

Counselor: **Part of becoming whole is overcoming the hurdles that you see have been there and you want to try to get over (reflecting of meanings).**

Client: Every day is a hurdle because I get faced with a new situation that I have to deal with and make a decision on my own.

Counselor: **How do you feel about making decisions on your own now (focusing)?**

Client: It feels good. It's getting better and better on a daily basis. It's been two years now so I've seen myself becoming progressively stronger every day and more confident in my decision making.

Counselor: **Well, we have a few minutes left and I think it is a good time to sum up what we have covered today. In a nutshell, you've been going through a divorce now for two years and you've experienced a lot of feelings during these two years as well as your marriage, including feeling abused, neglected, put down. You've experienced periods of depression and overwhelming confusion at times. Yet, now you find yourself starting to have the possibility of dating and doing new things for yourself and you feel very excited. Although you are wondering how your old feelings might play into what's happening now, yet it sounds like you are really striving for the light and I am happy for you (summarization).**

JOURNAL WRITING

The most important counseling "tool" is the *person* of the therapist. It is more important who the therapist is as a person than what techniques the therapist uses. In other words, good therapy cannot be reduced to good skills and techniques, but comes instead from the identity and integrity of the therapist. You are effective to the degree in which you know and trust yourself and are willing to become available and vulnerable in the services of your clients. To become such a therapeutic instrument, you will benefit greatly from exploring yourself through personal journal writing. Even when you are learning the language and skills of counseling, journal writing can help you engage in productive self-exploration, challenging you to clarify and develop personal beliefs, values, and feelings.

Themes or topics relevant to journal writing may include pre-existing listening skills, your personal strengths, growth edges and inspiring ideas, your inner dialogues with your struggles, and the significant experiences with your clients or with yourself that have brought you sharp insight into yourself as a therapist or a person.

The following examples are some edited excerpts of journal entries written by beginning counselors who have gone through the struggle of learning the language of counseling. "The book" that the trainees refer to in their journal entries is the draft of this book—*Individual Counseling: Skills and Techniques.*

Preface

This weekly journal has been very enlightening. In writing this, I have been forced to assess my progress while becoming a counselor. I began to internalize the skills we practiced. I have been constantly talking with myself, wishing I had a pen or paper, in the grocery store, in bed and even in the shower. I now listen to my friends' modes of conversation and analyze their communication. Most importantly, the journal has allowed me to listen to my internal voice. (W. F.)

Having an inner dialogue with myself was an inspiring experience. It brought new ideas and a better mental attitude. I can now connect the ideas behind the skills and understand why we are using each technique. The journal writing helps me explore my inner self and values. This was the most enjoyable part of the learning process in becoming a counselor. (C. M.)

Initial Stage Journal

When I role-played the client, I found it very uncomfortable at first talking to a virtual stranger about myself. I intended to role-play a problem at the first session, but quickly found myself relaxing and sharing my real-life problems. This really surprised me at first because I am usually very concerned about how I come across to people and don't want to appear foolish or vulnerable. These apprehensive feelings quickly subsided as I began to really enjoy talking about myself and my struggles. I found myself really looking forward to the session, both as the client and as the counselor. (E. P.)

After role-playing the client, I learned from my own fears that I need to be aware of the anxiety of a client who enters a counselor's office for the first time. Clients are more likely to feel awkward, and I need to be able to ease them into the process. The process of counseling needs to be explained so there is no misunderstanding about what the goals are. The explanation needs to be delivered with empathy so that it does not appear to be mechanical. (W. F.)

Before I read this book on counseling skills, I had always assumed that counseling was a form of giving advice and telling clients what to do. In my first lab session, I found myself giving my client advice. My client had talked about her husband verbally abusing her and her wanting to get a part-time job to help with finances and regain her sense of independence. I gave her advice. I told her to hang in there and pray to God for guidance and hope. I later learned that it was inappropriate and unhelpful to do that. I now know how unchecked presumptions about counseling can do disservice to my clients. (K. A.)

When I wrote out the taped sessions and used different color ink to represent myself and my client, I truly realized that I was taking up too much of the session with my own talk. I could easily see which sessions I tried to control and which I just let happen. I am finding that if I relax, let the session unfold, and don't push my own agenda, then I actually learn a lot from my client. (T. S.)

Watching myself counsel on video was a very humbling experience. When I watched myself, I realized that some of the things I thought I was doing, I wasn't actually doing. Often my reflections, probes, and other statements were not as clear as I wanted. This is because I had rushed to rehearse what I was going to say. Watching the videos, I learned that being a counselor is much different from being a teacher or being a friend. I must be conscious not to slip into these other roles while I am counseling. (I. L.)

Although many beginning counselors feel that they don't know what to say in the session, I sometimes feel myself at the opposite end of the spectrum: a wealth of ideas spring up. Now I need to learn how to temper my responses, to self-edit, to shorten my responses to facilitate the client. This is my most important area to improve right now. (P. K.)

My empathy for people began when I was a small child. I learned what it meant to grow up poor, without a father and without the ability to read until age nine. Many of my friends have been minorities, and I have witnessed many of the prejudices they have to deal with on a regular basis. These experiences taught me about humility, inner strength, being persistent, and that it is not right to judge other people based on their appearance, skin color, nationality, or socio-economic background. I have been able to express my empathy in my actions, but I have not been able to express it verbally until I learned the various reflective listening skills from this book . . . In learning how to verbalize empathy, I feel liberated. I have never liked the pat phrase, "I know what you are going through." Through this book I have been able to explore ways of verbalizing empathy. I am thankful for the chance to learn this very important skill. (T. S.)

I practiced at work the reflective listening skills that I learned from this book. It worked well! Yesterday, my boss was telling me about how his bosses at the parent company care about nothing but the bottom line. I reflected, "So, you are saying that in some ways it's good to feel the freedom, but on the other hand you feel they do not seem to care about us." He said "Exactly!" That was one of the first times I ever connected with my boss! (C. C.)

Counselor genuineness cannot be faked. The director of my son's preschool has a masters in counseling. Her skills are excellent but she seems phony. Her conversations seem canned and unnatural. By listening to her, I have learned that I must convey genuineness and compassion. I know that I honestly care and I hope that comes through. (W. F.)

Prior to practicing the skills I learned from this book, I intellectually understood the Rogerian ideals. Now I more fully appreciate their impact. Empathy, although difficult to maintain, must be a way of living. I must conscientiously remove the blinders of my own biases to more fully appreciate my client. Without a counselor's empathy, clients will continue to feel that their feelings are illegitimate. The absence of counselor empathy is the ultimate discounter. Without unconditional positive regard for the client, the client feels further devalued (P. K.)

Recently I was able to use some of the counseling skills I learned at work with an employee who got passed over for promotion. Our conversation extended to his future plans. I used an affirmation, stating "I really respect you for going back to school. It must be hard ... you work full time, you have a family." Then I stopped. Previously I had a tendency to show empathy and then keep talking. This time I kept it short. It worked! He seemed relieved that someone understood him. I felt like I was communicating my empathy to him. Prior to my learning these skills, I felt the empathy but was unable to show it because I am not very verbal. But once I learn something, I learn it well. (C. C.)

I now can see how questions are not the best way to allow clients to expand on their feelings; it basically cuts them off. Questions elicit cognitive answers and distract clients from continuing with the expression of feelings. Every issue needs to be worked out to its fullest and not left unfinished. Reflection of feelings or paraphrasing would be more effective. (E. B.)

I have become aware of some of my communication patterns and response styles. When people tell me about their issues or problems, I have a tendency to look for solutions or to give them advice before fully knowing the complexity of the issue. Another tendency is that I ask too many questions. I have now learned that this is not the best way to respond to someone. Through paraphrasing, reflection of feelings, and a little open probing, the client usually feels heard and validated and continues to explore to a deeper level. (C. S.)

I was afraid of making mistakes at first when I practiced these counseling skills. Then I realized that I need to allow myself to make mistakes in order to learn. So I attempted to try all the skills I learned with great gusto and abandon. At first some skills seemed very stilted and not genuine, but with practice I am able to incorporate them into my very being and as I become more comfortable with them, I become more genuine. (T. S.)

At the beginning I was really conscious about the video camera, but soon I got so involved with understanding my client that I began not to care about the camera. I usually am a strongly self-conscious person, shy and introverted. Now I realize that I do not have to label myself that way. Actually I have become comfortable with myself realizing that my self-consciousness is gone when I concentrate on what I am doing. Although I am shy, I have my valid insight to present to my client. See, I have got this confidence! (S. B.)

Having the chance to be a client has given me a little insight into how clients might feel as they begin a counseling relationship. I was scared, apprehensive, doubtful of getting anything out of it and embarrassed to share my personal life with a stranger. These are all feelings that my future clients will bring to me as well. Having had the opportunity to experience all these feelings first-hand will allow me to be a bit more compassionate and understanding of what my clients are experiencing. I will then work to portray that understanding, and strive to develop a relationship that will encourage the hope, sincerity, and risk-taking that will lead to successful change in my clients' lives. (E. P.)

Because English is not my native language (I learned to speak English a few years ago), my acquisition of the counseling skills is difficult because of the language barrier. To compensate for it, I have made extra efforts to practice at home. For example, I used the session tape to reenact the session again at home. After hearing what my client said, I stopped the tape and responded in different ways. This helped me understand my client better and gave me insight about my own response style. (S. B.)

Middle Stage Journal

The client does not need to be likable. I did not like my client initially. This concerned me. There were times I felt my empathy was faked. I wondered how counselors help their clients when they really don't like them. As the session progressed, I began to feel for my client, her pain, what she has experienced, and I hope I can find a way to make her feel better about herself. I now believe it is not essential to like a client to help a client. (W. F.)

The practice of case notes and theme analysis is very helpful in figuring out what direction my client needs to go and whether or not I am capable of offering that help. Learning that presenting problems are usually balloons was helpful in both of my clients' cases. It makes sense that my clients would want to know whether they can trust me before they decide to share further intimate thoughts and feelings with me. (T. S.)

When I discovered the themes and patterns in my client's struggles, I was able to use the higher influencing skills of immediacy and confrontation to help her recognize the conflicts, contradictions and other problems that became obvious to me but weren't to her . . . Often the themes and patterns in a person's life are more important to the problem than what appears to be the immediate issue. (I. L.)

I realized that my path of searching where to go in the session follows the theme analysis. I first test the theme, in its entirety, and in its specific parts. As I get more confident that the theme is correct, my responses are geared toward making that theme apparent to my client. I try to connect the thoughts that don't seem to have anything to do with each other, to show how dissimilar experiences may have similar components, to bring forth things that are barely seen consciously, and to draw out what may be thought but is spoken only by the tone of voice or the expression on the face. In other words, I try to make the unsaid become specific and spoken. (J. M.)

The theme analysis furnished me with a map as to the direction I needed to take to guide the client into self growth. With this map I could organize my thoughts before, during, and after each session. I felt as if I had control of the sessions, without controlling the client. I became more confident. (J. A.)

The middle stage of counseling seems to be the most difficult of all. My client was very comfortable during the initial stage, but was resistant to move to the next stage. This is where one can tell an effective counselor from an ineffective one. Breaking down the well-built walls people have used for a lifetime and getting them to acknowledge the walls' uselessness takes great skill. These defenses have managed to help the client survive. Despite clients wanting to change, they may not want to give up what is familiar and comfortable. All the counselor skills must be used to gently encourage the client to change. (W. F.)

I learned so much from doing case notes and theme analyses. I never thought to focus on my client's coping patterns, and this exercise helped me to recognize that their existence recreates and maintains many problems. By identifying and becoming aware of the coping patterns, the client becomes empowered to modify, change, or eliminate them. Basic case conceptualization gives me what really needs to be worked on—not just the presenting problems, but the whole person's behavioral, cognitive, affective behaviors. (E. B.)

I will pinpoint this week as my turning point in the lab. What a difference a session can make when it is opened with a summarization of the previous one! I have become confident in the realization that I can, indeed, be myself while implementing skills.(N. W.)

Even though some silence feels like hours, in reviewing my tapes I find that sometimes it is only a few seconds. I am learning to utilize silence and not feel that I have to take up every moment with a sound. I have learned to sometimes tell myself to shut up and listen to the silence and to use all of my senses to feel what is actually taking place. (T. S.)

The advanced skills are fascinating. The counselor is able to break all the rules to bring forth awareness for the client. I was raised to respect people's privacy and believe that if they want to share things with me, they will, and that it would be rude to delve deeper. However, advanced skills help me push past a client's defenses. (W. F.)

I like to use the advanced (influencing) skills and I am able to do that with my outside client. I would not feel as comfortable in using them if I had not practiced them in the lab or at home on my wife and on my stuffed animal. Making use of nonverbal cues has helped tremendously. I also like the use of growth edges (advanced empathy) very much. It offers clients a chance to feel and see their resiliency, which makes me feel good. (T. S.)

The counseling concept that brought me the most growth was the concept of looking for a client's strengths (growth edges and unique outcomes). It's so easy to see the problems; at the outset that was what I did with my client. Previously, instead of focusing on her determination and conscientiousness, I saw only her anxiety and sense of failure. When I began to rely on her strengths to guide the sessions, progress began to happen. Like the story of the man with only "one good tooth," all people have strengths that can be used to propel them to movement. Realizing this was moving to me. (M. H.)

At the beginning I did not understand why we should not join clients in their unconscious laughing. For me, laughing was one of the techniques used to lubricate social interaction. Now I have a sharper understanding of the meanings of nervous laughter. I tried to understand the meaning behind the client's laughter, rather than laughing with the client. (S. B.)

One of the most powerful concepts for me in regard to skills was the concept of advanced empathy. When I begin to distinguish between basic empathy, which reflects only obvious emotions, and the advanced empathy, which reflects the deepened awareness, a light bulb went on: "Such a powerful tool," I thought to myself. The fact that anyone can dwell so closely within another's issue, that one can see what that other person cannot see on his or her own, is compelling.(M. H.)

Counseling got more challenging with each session as I learned that not only did I have to listen to what my client was saying, but I had to "hear" her feelings, discover themes, and make connections between ideas that she wasn't perceiving. (I. L.)

Moving into the latter part of the middle stage, I began to feel more confident as I start to understand how reflection of feeling, such as "I sense how painful this is for you," can move into advanced empathy, such as "It sounds like you have a lot of regret, possibly guilt." Since I made the critical realization that I don't have to try to solve problems for my client, I no longer feel the need to give advice or to impart wisdom. (N. W.)

When I use confrontation in a gentle manner, it seems to help the counseling process. I especially like to use "confrontation of strength" since I like to accentuate the positive. Feedback-giving in the styles shown in this book has been very effective in building my client's self-efficacy. (T. S.)

Immediacy skill originally seemed almost rude and pushy. I was surprised to see how effective it was. Awareness definitely occurs as a result of the use of immediacy skills. When my peer counselor pointed out my laughter in my pain, I found it interesting, not rude. When I tried immediacy with my peer client, I noted her look of surprise. Immediacy seems to keep clients facing themselves honestly. (W. F.)

In today's session, I stayed away from exploring how my client felt when she was in obvious pain. I recognized that it is an issue of my own I need to work on. I am afraid of painful feelings. The observer and my client both noticed that I do not stay in the here-and-now. For example, I could have said at one point, "I see tears in your eyes," and I did not. In the moment I did think of what and how to say an empathic thing, but I lost the moment. I learned a valuable lesson today. (E. B.)

I was amazed at the power of reflexive questions. Specifically, I found that asking my client what her life would be like without all of her concerns helped her to open up and generate new meanings for herself. (A. M. K.)

I must develop the ability to give feedback to my client. Corrective feedback can be unintentionally hurtful if the wording is not proper. I must be careful to describe the client's behavior pattern before giving my reaction so that the feedback-giving is in the form of reaction to the behavior rather than an apparent judgment about the person. (A. G.)

I noticed that I was not able to deal with the feelings of my client because they were somehow foreign to me. I did not completely comprehend a white female client's feelings; therefore, instead of dealing with them directly, I intellectualized her feelings. How ironic I found it, to see myself as culturally incompetent. After all, it is usually the white counselors who are accused by multiculturalists of being culturally incompetent. Yet, the fault I saw in others was the fault that I discovered in myself. In becoming Hispanic-Centric for the past five years as a result of discrimination experiences, I seemed to have ignored the dominant discourse of society. In my mind, my discourse became dominant and I failed to acknowledge and in fact had stopped understanding the discourse of society. I became guilty of being blind. Just as I had decided that society had been blind to my feelings, I had failed to acknowledge the difference and maintain complete openness with my client. (A. G.)

One very important thing I learned, along with the knowledge of the skills, is how my own personal issues affect and interact with the effectiveness of skill usage. My tendency in my life has often been to avoid taking a strong stand and stating clearly what I want to say, to avoid making others angry. In my everyday life, this has allowed me to feel safe and to avoid conflicts with others. However, it has at the same time kept me from feeling a sense of power that is essential to my personal growth as an adult woman. Although I was somewhat aware of this communication tendency in me, I did not realize how pervasive it is and how much it would effect my skills as a therapist. Through my work with clients, I am becoming more and more aware of how important it is to be clear, concise, and sometimes direct, particularly in a therapeutic setting. (C. C.)

I am motivated to extend my outside reading so that I can acquaint myself with different core issues that various clients struggle with. (Y. O.)

I found doing the contextual analysis to be quite helpful for me to better understand what societal influences may shape the client to maintain her current behavior. (A. M. K.)

Later Stage Journal

This will be the fun stage. Progress can be seen. It will be rewarding to see the client move toward goals. Role-reversal, directives, and other interventions are more work for the client than the counselor. (W. F.)

I like to use directives, in particular awareness homework, experiential teaching, and attention suggestions. I feel at home with these interventions. (T. S.)

The counseling interaction is a delicate privilege afforded to the counselor. The empty chair intervention technique crystallized for me the great ethical and personal care that must be taken by the counselor. Leading a client to such emotional vulnerability is both fascinating and humbling. Yet in the hands of a therapist who has other agendas and personal objectives, this can be dangerous. (P. K.)

My best session with my client was when I practiced the empty chair technique. My client had been talking about her mother-in-law and how difficult it was to please her. My client also talked about how in her culture the mother-in-law picks out the bride for her son. She is kind of a queen mother. So I had my client confront her mother-in-law using the empty chair technique. I was able to see what a powerful technique this is. I could see a change in my client. Afterward, my client talked of how much better she felt. I could see relief on her face. (M. K.)

While practicing the empty chair technique I was very touched by a member of the triad who broke into tears. I wanted very much to stop the session to relieve her from the tears because working with tearful clients is very difficult for me. After the session, I spoke with her and understand the power of this practice. She said that it was truly helpful to fully experience the emotions as she had. (N. D.)

I was mesmerized by the empty chair exercises performed by both my client and another classmate under the guidance of our professor. What a powerful intervention technique! I am feeling more and more, largely resulting from the emotions generated by this class, that I have made the right decision in returning to school, this school, and studying counseling. I'm thrilled to be living in the present, soaking in the learning and experiences that this class has provided. These warm emotions provide the necessary outlet for my sensitivity, which, too often, remains only within. I find myself to be coming out of my shell, being much less self-centered, less worried about pride, more interested in helping, more at ease and more proud of and happy to be who I am. (N. W.)

One of the best lecture sessions was when our professor demonstrated the empty chair technique with one of my classmates. The client's emotions so touched me that I broke into tears along with her. I realized what a powerful tool the technique can be. As I looked around the room, everyone else seemed touched and moved by the experience. My client expressed a wish to use this technique in our session. Because I was so taken with the idea of the empty chair, I asked my professor to do the technique with me. As we did the empty chair, I felt for the first time as a client that I could express my feelings without any hesitation or fear. I brought some unfinished business to the surface. I was surprised that I could focus on my emotions and express them without difficulty. This was the most rewarding experience that I had as a client. My professor was a very gentle coach who guided me with encouragement and patience. I see now that there are constructive ways to lead a client to feel emotion and liberation. (C. M.)

Even with my best friends I have not really had a chance to learn as much about them as I learned about my lab client even in a short time. (I. L.)

As I read through my journal over the past several weeks, I see how the relationship with my client began to develop and grow into something that was truly trusting and safe for both of us. I was surprised by this occurrence as I did not expect this to happen in the somewhat artificial setting of the lab. The relationship was somewhat stilted and uncomfortable at the beginning but truly changed its form over the next several weeks as we covered more ground and discussed deeper issues. The growth was also facilitated by writing the case notes and case conceptualization, because the writing helped me integrate and assimilate what we were accomplishing in the sessions. (C. C.)

Termination Stage Journal

With termination, I found that it was good that I laid the groundwork three sessions before we ended. Neither of us really wanted to terminate the counseling process, though. (T. S.)

During this stage, we ask the client to evaluate the process. Requesting a client's opinion and feedback can be frightening, yet the client's comments help me improve as a counselor. The client may also feel empowered by the request. This is a way to show a client that the counselor values his or her opinion. It was interesting to witness how difficult saying goodbye was for our triad. One of us was laughing and playing tricks to avoid saying goodbye. Another was angry. I was quick and to-the-point. Ending relationships, including therapeutic ones, is difficult. (W. F.)

The final session was uplifting and we found it difficult to terminate. We were both thirsty for more. Now that we have said goodbye, I feel some sense of loss. Ending this relationship was more difficult then we imagined, but we did it with mutual respect. (C. M.)

I am a bit disappointed in myself for not becoming more immediate during our final sessions. When I sensed my client's tension, had I said, "It seems like there's only so far you'll let me go," a more deepening response might have followed. (N. W.)

At the final session in the training, I found it very difficult to terminate with my peer counselor. When I wanted to say goodbye, I found myself playing pranks and jokes. I did not want to say goodbye, again. Three weeks ago, I had to ask my mother to take my 23-month-old daughter to my country for four months. I still haven't gotten over her absence. And now I have to say goodbye to my peer counselor. I feel a sense of loss. To separate from this therapeutic relationship feels like grieving a relative's death. I finally dealt with my unfinished business; my peer counselor and I said our goodbye in a mutual and respective manner. (K. A.)

I felt deeply moved and gratified that I was able to help. During the final session I felt a very strong emotion in the room between my client and myself as we said goodbye. My client told me how much she was going to miss our sessions and there was a sadness in her words and voice that I felt as well. (A. M. K.)

Epilogue Journal

This skill training has been one I love the most so far. I spent a lot of time practicing, reading, reviewing each tape, writing out case notes, theme analysis, and critiques, thinking up strategies and techniques to use, putting my thoughts and experiences into my journal, and generally working hard and putting a lot of effort into it. The amount of time and effort I put forth really shows in my progress. I feel good about my skill and developmental growth. (T. S.)

Over the past 12 weeks I have changed. Instead of assuming I know much about interpersonal communication, I realize I have much to learn. I am encouraged, though, by my progress through the process, the practice of skills, and the personal growth that I experienced during the training period. I am confident that over time I will eventually move from the ranks of the beginner to the skilled therapist. (M. H.)

I am very pleased that we went through all the skills because I learn best by doing. I would have felt cheated if we had not covered the advanced skills and intervention techniques. One of my goals is to keep this book on my night stand and re-read a few pages every night until I have absorbed the entire scope. (T. S.)

The challenge of skill training is very true. Initially everything seemed so overwhelming, but now I feel that I have come a long way and I feel good about my skill development. I am going to miss this training process, my colleagues, the practice sessions, the feedback, and my professor. (T. S.)

This counseling skill training experience has helped me communicate differently with individuals in my life. For example, when speaking with friends, I am aware of feelings and emotions that they have been expressing but I never took notice of until I took this course. (Y. O.)

Analysis of myself as a counselor has been the best teaching tool for me. I have left this training course with renewed energy in attempting to comprehend the world from different perspectives. (A. G.)

In closing, I am thrilled to have been a part of this increasingly challenging course. In experiencing the peaks and valleys that it has generated, I'm proud to say that I have become more attuned in my everyday life. I will remember this skill training experience and these months as critical stepping stones upon my journey toward actualizing my potentials. (N. W.)

APPENDIX C

PRELIMINARY INFORMATION FORM

Preliminary Information Form

North Shore Counseling Center

All information will be kept confidential.

Name: _____ Date: _____

Address: _____

_____

Phone: (home) _____(work) _____

OK to leave messages: Yes _____No _____

Date of Birth: _____Gender: Female_____Male _____

Marital status: single_____ married_____ divorced_____ widowed_____ cohabiting_____

Ethnic background: _____

Occupation/Work: _____Referral source: _____

Have you ever participated in previous counseling? Yes _____ No _____

If yes, at_____

Please check those issues that concern you (check all that may apply):

_____ anxiety	_____ relational concerns	_____ alcohol concerns
_____ depression	_____ sexual concerns	_____ drug concerns
_____ anger	_____ sexual assault/abuse	_____ eating concerns
_____ death/grief	_____ suicidal thoughts	_____ family issues
_____ Other: _____		

From the list above, circle the one most important issue.

APPENDIX D

COUNSELOR SELF-CRITIQUE

One way to promote your professional growth is self-monitoring—self-critique. Critiquing your own skill response is one example. Self-critique helps you develop a persistent attitude and enhances your ability to differentiate effective responses from ineffective ones and to create strategies that will produce preferred skills. When you critique yourself, you should focus on your performance, not on your personal attributes.

EXAMPLE OF COUNSELOR SELF-CRITIQUE

Throughout the session, I tried to utilize some advanced skills in addition to the basic skills. I also strived to be briefer in my responses and was at times effective; however, I still see room for growth in this area. In any event, I feel I was effective in working with the client and understand the problem from her perspective.

Effective Responses

The following responses are those that I consider to be effective in helping my client explore her issues. These are the responses I feel I can continue to use:

Reflection of feelings

Client: "It's not just that my mom is not there for me, because she is, really. It's just that she's not showing her appreciation for everything that I have done for her as far as planning her wedding is concerned. She is so caught up with her life now, which is of course understandable, because this wedding is a big deal in her life and a big step for her. I still feel she could show a little appreciation for everything I have done for her."

199

Counselor: **"I sense that you are feeling unappreciated and this is very troubling to you."**

Advanced Empathy

Client: "Right, and also because her friends are here and she is not going to want to spend her weekend with us. She will want to visit with her sister and the church people. She will probably just have breakfast with us and spend the rest of her time elsewhere. Spending time to me means spending the day together, not just a couple of hours."

Counselor: **"Although you have said that you feel your mother has not totally forgotten about you, I get the sense that you have this underlying fear of being forgotten and being put on the back burner."**

Client: " Yes, it is painful. I don't know how much pain. It's just that I am not letting myself feel any pain because I am letting the anger take over."

Counselor: **"Even though the anger is there, I sense that underneath there is still that feeling of being hurt and lost."**

Immediacy

Client: "I wonder, does she realize how much she has meant to me and how much she has inspired me? I wonder, does she know that? So I am thinking about writing her, about sending her a card, so that she can be aware of how much I miss her. (The client began to cry, while at the same time, smiled.)

Counselor: **"I see tears in your eyes, and I see a smile. Could you tell me what you are feeling right now?"**

Advanced Empathy and Perception Checking

Counselor: **"There seems to be a inner struggle between having your needs met and, at the same time, being happy with your mother's decision to embark upon her new life. I sense that, despite your mother's decision to move away, you still want her close by. Am I correct in describing the way you are experiencing it?"**

Summarization

Counselor: **"Again, we have tapped into some of the difficulties you are experiencing, and we have identified the conflicting feelings that you have concerning your needs and those of your mother."**

Client: "Yeah, we have, and I think these feelings will continue for a while. However, now I will grow. I don't see this as affecting me long term. It's just that it's so new, and it is so fresh."

Advanced Empathy

Counselor: **"In spite of all that's going on in your life, I sense an inner strength and determination."**

Client: "Yeah, these are probably the best qualities I have. I don't see myself as needing someone for my strength. It's just a need for myself."

Ineffective Responses and Alternative Responses

The following are the responses that I considered to be ineffective. To improve my skills, I have thought of what other alternative responses I may use to replace them if given a second chance:

Client: "I have always reached my goals, the goals I set for myself. I see myself as selfish because being selfish means not seeing my mother's needs. I am only thinking about myself and that is not fair because I am not considering how she is feeling."

Counselor: "I hear you say that you are aware of your needs, and I hear your concern for your mother's needs, yet I still sense an inner cry that says, 'I want my mother to be here with me, regardless of whatever else is happening.'"

This was ineffective because I did not seem to clearly communicate to my client the core meaning I intended. In addition, I should have done so in fewer words. Alternative responses would be:

"Despite your feelings about your needs, I sense that you are experiencing some feelings of guilt. Is this the way you are experiencing it?" (advanced empathy and perception checking)

"I sense that, although you are upset about your mother's moving away, you believe that you are not supposed to feel that way." (advanced empathy)

Client: "I am still feeling angry at her, because at the reception after the wedding, she was paying a lot of attention to other people and ignoring us. It felt almost as if she was trying to impress them. It was almost as if she had to put up a front. That really made me angry. She is a great person, and I don't think she should have to be different. She took a lot of pictures of other people, but what about us?"

Counselor: **"Um-hum."**

Client: "So, now she has a new family, and that's fine and dandy, but she shouldn't throw away her old family because we were there for her when they were not. So, that made me really mad."

Counselor: I am sensing that not only did you feel pushed aside per se, but also the fact that she was so caught up in being something she is not in trying to impress other people, is disturbing to you, and you are wondering why she should try to impress other people when you love her for herself and she doesn't have to impress you."

I feel this was ineffective because the paraphrasing was too wordy and did not bring the client to a deeper level of self-discovery. Alternative responses would be:

"You feel hurt because your mother appeared to be caught up with everyone else in her wedding." (reflection of feeling)

"I hear anger, and I sense pain in your voice." (immediacy)

Client: "I guess I am more on my own as far as planning for a sitter and taking care of things. I knew this was going to happen. I anticipated it happening, but not like this. I didn't expect it to happen this way."

Counselor: I sense that you are afraid she is not going to be there for you at all."

I feel this is ineffective because it did not convey how much her mother means to my client. Alternative responses:

"The thought of losing your mother as an integral part of your life is unsettling to you." (advanced empathy)

"Going through life without having your mother close by as a support seems quite disturbing for you." (advanced empathy)

Future Skill Development

To be more effective, I would like to continue to develop some of the more advanced skills, such as immediacy, confrontation, and feedback-giving to better help my clients not only gain deeper insights by addressing their problems, but also become more aware of their inner resources and, subsequently, empower themselves.

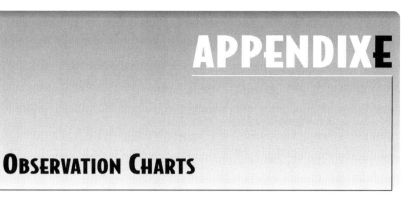

APPENDIX E

OBSERVATION CHARTS

A nother way to increase self-awareness of skill development is by using the observation charts. You or the observer may use the following chart to keep track of your response style. This can be useful in making you aware of your strengths and weaknesses in developing counseling skills.

Use of Skills

Basic Empathic Skills +	Counts	Observation Comments
Inquiry Skills		
Paraphrasing		
Reflection of Feelings		
Affirmation		
Summarization		
Perception Checking		
Reflection of Meaning		
Pacing		
Focusing		
Probing		
Clarifying Statements		

Advanced/Influencing Skills	Counts	Observation Comments
Advanced Empathy: Implicit Feelings		
Advanced Empathy: Identifying Patterns		
Advanced Empathy: Connecting Islands		
Advanced Empathy: Growth Edges		
Advanced Empathy: Graphic Language		
Advanced Empathy: Succession		
Counselor Self-Disclosure		
Immediacy		
Confrontation		
Feedback-Giving		

Use of Intervention Techniques

Intervention Techniques	Counts	Observation Comments
Directives		
Parts Dialogue		
Empty Chair		
Reflexive Questions		
Narrative Steps		
Body Awareness		
The "Yes" Set		
The "No" Set		

REFERENCES

Bandler, R. (1979). *Frogs into princes: Neuro-linguistic programming.* Moab, Utah: Real People Press.

Bandura, A. (1982). Self-efficacy mechanism in human agency. *American Psychologist, 37,* 122–147.

Barker, P. (1985). *Using metaphors in psychotherapy.* New York: Brunner/Mazel.

Benson, H. (1975). *The relaxation response.* New York: Avon.

Brammer, L. M., & Macdonald, G. (1996). *Helping relationship: Process and skills.* Boston: Allyn and Bacon.

Brickman, P., Rabinowitz, V. C., Karuza, J., Coates, D., Cohn, E., & Kidder, L. (1982). Four models of helping and coping. *American Psychologist, 37,* 368–384.

Carkhuff, R. R., & Pierce, R. M. (1975). *Trainer's guide: The art of helping.* Amherst, MA: Human Resource Development Press.

Cudney, M. R., & Hardy, R. E. (1991). *Self-defeating behaviors.* New York: Harper Collins.

Daldrup, R. J., Beutler, L. E., Engle, D., & Greenberg, L. S. (1988). *Focused expressive psychotherapy: Feeling the overcontrolled patient.* New York: Guilford.

Dolan, Y. M. (1985). *A path with a heart: Ericksonian utilization with resistant and chronic clients.* New York: Brunner/Mazel.

Egan, G. (1976). *Interpersonal living: A skill/contract approach to human relations training in groups.* Monterey, CA: Brooks/Cole.

Egan, G. (1994). *The skilled helper.* Pacific Grove, CA: Brooks/Cole.

Fisch, R., Weakland, J. H., & Segal, L. (1982). *The tactics of change: Doing therapy briefly.* San Francisco, CA: Jossey-Bass.

Freedman, J., & Combs, G. (1996). *Narrative therapy.* New York: Norton.

Garner, A. (1991). *Conversationally speaking.* Los Angeles: Lowell House.

Greenberg, L. S., Rice, L. N., & Elliott, R. (1993). *Facilitating emotional change: The moment by moment process.* New York: Guilford.

Griffith, J. L., & Griffith, M. E. (1994). *The body speaks: Therapeutic dialogues for mind-body problems.* New York: Basic Books.

Hanb, T. N. (1991). *Peace is every step: The path of mindfulness in everyday life.* New York: Bantam Books.

Haley, J. (1976). *Problem-solving therapy.* San Francisco: Jossey-Bass.

Keel, L., & Brown, S. (July 1999). Professional disclosure statement. *Counseling Today, 14.*

Kiesler, D. J., & Van Denburg, T. F. (1993). Therapeutic impact disclosure: A last taboo in psychoanalytic theory and practice. *Clinical Psychology & Psychotherapy, 1,* 3–13.

Long, V. O. (1996). *Communication skills in helping relationships.* Pacific Grove: Brooks/Cole.

Martin, D. G. (1983). *Counseling and therapy skills.* Monterey, CA: Brooks/Cole.

Meier, S. T. (1983). Toward a theory of burnout. *Human Relations, 36,* 899–910.

Meier, S. T., & Davis, S. R. (1993). *The elements of counseling.* Pacific Grove, CA: Brooks/Cole.

Miller, W. R., & Rollnick, S. (1991). *Motivational interviewing: Preparing people to change addictive behavior.* New York: Guilford.

Morrison, J. (1993). *The first interview: A guide for clinicians.* New York: Guilford.

National Mental Health Association Commission on the Prevention of Mental-Emotional Disabilities (1986). *The Prevention of Mental-Emotional Disabilities: Report of the National Mental Health Association Commission on the Prevention of Mental-Emotional Disabilities.* Alexandria, VA: National Mental Health Association.

Neimeyer, R. A. (1996). Process interventions for the constructivist psychotherapist. In H. Rosen & K. T. Kuehlwein (Eds.) *Constructing Realities: Meaning-Making Perspectives for Psychotherapists.* San Francisco: Jossey-Bass.

Robbins, A. (1986). *Unlimited power.* New York: Fawcett Columbine.

Schloff, L., & Yudkin, M. (1991). *Smart speaking.* New York: Penguin Books.

Smith, E. W. (1985). *The body in psychotherapy.* Jefferson, NC: McFarland & Co.

Sue, D. W. (1990). Culture-specific strategies in counseling: A conceptual framework. *Professional Psychology: Research and Practice, 21,* 424–433.

Teyber, E. (1997). *Interpersonal process in psychotherapy: A relational approach.* Pacific Grove, CA: Brooks/Cole.

Tomm, K. (1987) Interventive interviewing: Part II. *Family Process, 26,* 167–183.

Tomm, K. (1988) Interventive interviewing: Part III. *Family Process, 27,* 1–15.

White, M. (1989). The externalization of the problem and the re-authoring of lives and relationships. In M. White *Selective Paper,* 5–28.

Yalom, I. D. (1983). *Inpatient group psychotherapy.* New York: Basic Books.

Yalom, I. D. (1995). *The theory and practice of group psychotherapy.* New York: Basic Books.

Zukerman, E. L. (1997). *The paper office.* New York: Guilford.

INDEX